LE CREUSET DUTCH OVEN FOR BEGINNERS

Step-by-Step Guide to Using, Cleaning, and Cooking Perfect Meals in Your Enameled Cast Iron Pot

OLIVIA O. HARTWELL

Copyright © 2025 by Olivia O. Hartwell

All rights reserved. No part of this publication may be reproduced, distributed, or transmitted in any form or by any means, including photocopying, recording, or other electronic or mechanical methods, without the prior written permission of the publisher, except in the case of brief quotations embodied in critical reviews and certain other noncommercial uses permitted by copyright law.

Disclaimer

This book, *Le Creuset Dutch Oven for Beginners: Step-by-Step Guide to Using, Cleaning, and Cooking Perfect Meals in Your Enameled Cast Iron Pot*, is an independent publication created for educational and informational purposes only. It is designed to help readers understand the general use, care, and cooking techniques associated with enameled cast iron Dutch ovens.

All brand names, product names, and trademarks mentioned are the property of their respective owners. Le Creuset® is a registered trademark of Le Creuset Group AG. This book is not authorized, sponsored, endorsed, or affiliated in any way with Le Creuset Group AG or any of its subsidiaries or representatives. Any references to the Le Creuset brand are made solely for descriptive and educational purposes, as part of a general discussion on enameled cast iron cookware.

This book should not be considered a substitute for official product manuals, safety guidelines, or warranty information provided by Le Creuset or any other manufacturer. Readers are advised to consult the manufacturer's official resources for product-specific care, maintenance, and warranty procedures.

By reading and using this guide, you acknowledge that you have read, understood, and agreed to the terms of this disclaimer.

TABLE OF CONTENTS

HOW TO USE THIS BOOK
INTRODUCTION
CHAPTER 1
THE STORY BEHIND LE CREUSET
- A Century of Craftsmanship
- What Makes Le Creuset Different
- The Science of Enameled Cast Iron

CHAPTER 2
ANATOMY OF A DUTCH OVEN
- Sizes, Shapes, and Capacities Explained
- Signature vs. Classic: What's the Difference?
- Choosing the Right Dutch Oven for Your Cooking Style

CHAPTER 3
BEFORE THE FIRST USE
- How to Inspect and Prepare Your Dutch Oven
- The Dos and Don'ts of Preheating
- Understanding Heat Retention and Distribution

CHAPTER 4
MASTERING THE BASICS
- How to Sear, Braise, Bake, and Roast
- Proper Techniques for Stovetop and Oven Cooking
- Temperature Control Tips for Perfect Results

CHAPTER 5
EVERYDAY COOKING TECHNIQUES
- Slow Cooking Made Simple
- How to Make Soups, Stews, and Sauces
- One-Pot Meals for Busy Days
- Baking Bread in Your Dutch Oven

CHAPTER 6
ADVANCED COOKING TIPS
- Layering Flavors for Depth
- Deglazing Like a Chef
- Using Your Dutch Oven for Frying, Poaching, and Simmering

CHAPTER 7

CLEANING YOUR LE CREUSET
- Daily Cleaning Steps
- Removing Stains and Burnt Residue
- What Not to Do When Cleaning
- Reviving Dull Enamel

CHAPTER 8
PROTECTING AND STORING
- How to Prevent Chipping and Scratches
- Proper Storage Methods
- Handling Lids, Knobs, and Accessories Safely

CHAPTER 9
TROUBLESHOOTING COMMON PROBLEMS
- Why Food Sticks (and How to Fix It)
- Discoloration and Stain Removal Tips
- When to Contact Le Creuset Support

CHAPTER 10
EASY EVERYDAY RECIPES
- Classic Beef Stew
- Creamy Chicken and Vegetables
- Simple Homemade Chili
- No-Knead Artisan Bread

CHAPTER 11
WEEKEND & SPECIAL OCCASION DISHES
- Coq au Vin (French Wine-Braised Chicken)
- Braised Short Ribs with Red Wine
- Baked Mac & Cheese
- Dutch Oven Lasagna

CHAPTER 12
HEALTHY & MODERN RECIPES
- Quinoa Vegetable Stew
- Mediterranean Chickpea Curry
- Roasted Vegetable Ratatouille
- Whole-Grain Dutch Oven Bread

CHAPTER 13
ACCESSORIES AND ADD-ONS
- Must-Have Tools and Utensils
- Silicone vs. Wooden Spoons: Which Is Best?
- Recommended Cookware Companions

CHAPTER 14
CARING FOR YOUR LE CREUSET FOR LIFE
- Long-Term Maintenance Habits
- Warranty, Repairs, and Restorations
- Passing It Down: Making Your Dutch Oven a Family Heirloom

CONCLUSION

APPENDICES
- Appendix A — Temperature Conversion Chart
- Appendix B — Cooking Times & Heat Levels Guide
- Appendix C — Cleaning Cheat Sheet
- Appendix D — Resources & Further Reading

HOW TO USE THIS BOOK

Whether you've just unboxed your very first Dutch oven or you've had one sitting in your kitchen for years waiting for inspiration, this book is your go-to companion for getting the most out of one of the most versatile and beloved pieces of cookware ever made.

This guide is designed to take you from absolute beginner to confident cook—step by step, chapter by chapter. You'll learn not only *how* to use your Le Creuset Dutch oven, but *why* it works the way it does, so you can make smarter, more satisfying meals every single time.

Here's how to get the most out of this book:

---

1. Start at the Beginning—Even if You Think You Know the Basics

If you're new to enameled cast iron, the early chapters will help you understand what makes your Le Creuset special. You'll learn about its design, materials, and the science behind its remarkable heat retention and even cooking. Even experienced cooks will discover a few surprises about the way these pots handle heat and moisture.

---

2. Follow the Step-by-Step Flow

Each chapter builds naturally on the one before it. You'll begin with setup and seasoning (or lack thereof, since Le Creuset comes ready to use!), then move through cooking techniques, cleaning, troubleshooting, and care. The recipes toward the end of the book are intentionally chosen to help you *practice what you've learned*—starting simple and growing more creative as you go.

---

3. Use the Subsections as Quick References

Within each chapter, you'll find focused sections on topics like preheating, temperature control, slow cooking, and cleaning methods. These are written in plain, approachable language so you can easily return to them whenever you need a refresher. Think of them as your built-in "kitchen notes."

4. Don't Skip the Appendices

The appendices at the back of the book are packed with handy quick-reference tools. From temperature conversions and cooking times to a cleaning cheat sheet and suggested resources, these sections are designed to make your everyday cooking smoother and more intuitive. Keep them bookmarked—you'll use them often.

5. Experiment and Make It Your Own

Your Dutch oven is incredibly forgiving and adaptable. Use this book as a guide, but don't be afraid to explore your own variations. Once you're comfortable with the basics, you'll find yourself improvising with confidence—tossing in fresh herbs, adjusting heat levels, and discovering your own favorite one-pot meals.

6. Learn from Mistakes and Celebrate Wins

Cooking is both science and art. If something sticks, burns slightly, or turns out differently than you expected, don't worry—it's part of the process. Later chapters on troubleshooting and cleaning will help you recover from common missteps, while maintenance and storage tips ensure your Dutch oven lasts for decades.

7. Keep It Close to the Kitchen

This isn't the kind of book meant to sit on a shelf. Keep it open on your counter, sticky-note your favorite sections, and let it get a little flour-dusted or splattered with sauce. That's a sign you're really using it—the way it was meant to be used.

By the time you reach the final chapter, you'll not only know how to make classic and modern recipes in your Le Creuset, but you'll also understand *why* they work so beautifully in this type of cookware. You'll have the confidence to take on everything from a quick weeknight meal to a slow-simmered Sunday feast.

So take a deep breath, lift that heavy lid with pride, and get ready to fall in love with your Dutch oven. Every great home cook starts somewhere—and for you, that "somewhere" begins right here.

INTRODUCTION

If you're holding this book, chances are you've either just unboxed your very first Le Creuset Dutch oven—or you've owned one for years but never quite learned how to use it to its full potential. Either way, congratulations. You're now the proud owner of one of the most iconic, dependable, and downright beautiful pieces of cookware ever made.

A Le Creuset Dutch oven isn't just another pot; it's a kitchen workhorse that can do almost everything. From slow-cooked stews to crusty homemade bread, from perfectly tender roasts to one-pot pasta dinners—it's the kind of tool that can make everyday meals taste special. But like any great tool, it performs best when you understand how it works and how to take care of it.

That's where this book comes in.

My goal in writing *Le Creuset Dutch Oven for Beginners* is simple: to help you feel confident and inspired every time you reach for your Dutch oven. Whether you're learning how to use it safely on the stovetop, figuring out how to clean it without damaging the enamel, or experimenting with your first braised dish, this guide will walk you through every step.

You'll find clear explanations, practical tips, and straightforward instructions written for real home cooks—no fancy jargon, no intimidating techniques. You'll also find delicious, foolproof recipes designed to help you build skill and confidence one meal at a time.

Throughout these pages, we'll talk about what makes Le Creuset cookware special, how to use it properly, and how to care for it so it lasts for decades. You'll learn how to manage heat, avoid common mistakes (like overheating or scratching the enamel), and troubleshoot small issues before they become big ones. And once you've mastered the basics, you'll be ready to explore all the ways your Dutch oven can simplify and elevate your cooking.

Think of this book as your kitchen companion—part instruction manual, part cookbook, part conversation between fellow cooks. I'll share the know-how you need, but I'll also share the joy of using something that turns everyday ingredients into something truly memorable.

By the time you finish this guide, you'll not only know how to use your Le Creuset Dutch oven—you'll know how to make it *yours*. You'll have the confidence to improvise, the skills to care for it properly, and the inspiration to cook with heart.

So grab your Dutch oven, tie on your apron, and let's get started. The secret to great cooking is already in your hands.

CHAPTER 1

THE STORY BEHIND LE CREUSET

From the moment you first see that glossy enamel-coloured pot sitting proudly on the stove, you sense there's something more than just metal and function at work. There's heritage. There's craft. There's story. For many of us, owning a piece from Le Creuset isn't just about having cookware—it's about joining a tradition of cooking, of kitchen gatherings and heirlooms passed down. That first swirl of sauce, that first braise simmering under a snug lid—when you bring home a Le Creuset Dutch oven, you bring home a little bit of that legacy.

In this chapter we'll step back and explore the story behind Le Creuset—the company, the craft, the ethos that underpins every piece. Why has this brand endured for so long? What sets it apart? And when you look closely at the materials and the design, what science makes it perform so well in your kitchen? By understanding where your Dutch oven comes from, you'll not only appreciate what's in your hands, you'll gain insight into how to treat it, how to get the most out of it, and why it's worth the investment.

Whether you bought your Dutch oven brand new or it was passed down to you, whether you're cooking your first stew or planning to bake bread in it—knowing the roots of the cookware deepens your connection, helps you cook more confidently, and invites you to treat it as more than just a pot. So let's begin by travelling back to 1925, to a foundry in northern France, to two industrialists and a bold idea that has echoed through kitchens for a century.

A Century of Craftsmanship

In 1925, in the small town of Fresnoy-le-Grand in northern France, two men—Armand De Saegher (a Belgian casting specialist) and Octave Aubecq (a Belgian enamelling expert)—founded a company that would become Le Creuset. They chose that region strategically—it sat at the junction of transportation routes for cast iron, coke, and sand, the raw materials integral to their plan. Together they cast and enameled cookware in a process that was new for the time—combining heavy duty cast iron with vibrant, tough enamel finishes. The result was the first "cocotte" (French-style oven, or Dutch oven equivalent) produced by Le Creuset in 1925, in their now-iconic "Flame" orange colour.

From the very beginning, their ambition wasn't simply to produce another pot—it was to create a pot that cooked better, endured longer and delighted the eye. They believed that cookware should belong on the table, not hidden away in the cupboard. Over the decades that followed, Le Creuset grew steadily, introducing new colourways, expanding their product range, acquiring other foundries, and refining their processes—but always anchored in that original foundry and craft. In 2015 they celebrated their 90-year milestone by marking that their pieces have been part of countless memories, from daily dinners to festive gatherings.

What is remarkable is the continuity of their manufacturing approach. Even in a time when many cookware brands shifted to mass production overseas, Le Creuset's cast-iron enameled line is still produced in the same town and same foundry where it began. That craftsmanship mindset—metal cast by sand molds, enamel applied in layers, each piece individually inspected—is a big part of why owning a Le Creuset feels different. It's not just the performance, it's the lineage, the idea that you are cooking in something born from decades of refinement.

When you consider your Dutch oven, think of it as a 100-year-old idea refined in your hands today. The weight of the lid, the glossy finish, the feeling when you turn the knob—those are tactile echoes of that history. And that history invites respect: the craftsmanship asks that you treat it with intention, that you care for it so that it, too, becomes part of your kitchen story for decades.

What Makes Le Creuset Different

So, what exactly elevates Le Creuset from "nice cookware" to something many consider a lifetime investment? It's more than just branding. Here are the key differentiators you'll want to internalize as you learn to use your Dutch oven.

First and foremost: the combination of heavy-duty cast iron and high-quality enamel. Many cookware pieces might claim durability or specialty coatings. But Le Creuset's design begins with cast iron—which is already excellent at absorbing and holding heat—and layers it with enamel that resists rust, eliminates the need for seasoning, and adds aesthetic versatility. The result is cookware that behaves differently from typical cheap pots. As their own website states: "Authentic and iconic for 100 years and counting … they're heirlooms in the making."

Second: the manufacturing process and attention to detail. At Le Creuset's French foundry, each piece still goes through a sand-casting process, followed by finishing, enamelling, multiple quality-control stages, and colour matching. That level of oversight means two things for you as a user: 1) the cookware will behave consistently in the kitchen; 2) you're buying product backed by decades of refinement, not a "lowest cost" manufacture. From the full-sized Dutch oven to the lid knob, even the small details are considered.

Third: the brand's identity as both functional and beautiful. That first "Flame" orange cocotte in 1925 set the tone. Today there are dozens of colours, subtle finishes, special editions—but the cookware is still built to perform. The provenance is real. The foundry remains in France, and the brand still emphasizes heritage, craft and performance. This combination—function plus form—is rare. Many pots might offer one or the other, but with Le Creuset you get confidently that it will cook well and look good doing it.

Fourth: the brand's reputation and community. Over the years, home cooks, professional chefs and collectors alike have embraced these pieces. They show up in kitchens where meals matter. They are passed down. They build memories. That communal trust matters. When you own and use one of these pieces, you join that community—it's part of why the "for beginners" orientation of this book matters: because while many people buy the pot for its look, the real magic happens when you learn to use it well.

Finally, the warranty, the longevity and the value retention: many users find that when they care for their Le Creuset cookware properly, it lasts for decades. That level of durability means that it becomes part of your kitchen narrative rather than a temporary purchase.

So when you pick up your Dutch oven and place it on the stove, you're not just cooking—you're continuing a tradition of quality, intention and design. In the chapters ahead you'll learn exactly how to treat this piece so it serves you well; but it's helpful, at the outset, to appreciate what sets it apart.

The Science of Enameled Cast Iron

Now that you know about the heritage and craftsmanship, let's take a closer look at what's happening under the surface—literally. The material science of enameled cast iron explains why your Dutch oven heats the way it does, retains warmth for so long, and behaves differently from lightweight cookware. It also explains how to use it intelligently, how to avoid mistakes and how to care for it properly.

At its core, your piece is cast iron—known for excellent heat retention. Cast iron has a high thermal mass, meaning it takes time to heat but once it does, it stays hot. This makes it ideal for slow cooking, braising, stewing—recipes where consistent, sustained heat matters. What the enamel does is create a smooth, non-porous outer layer (and often interior layer) that bonds to the cast iron and provides several advantages: it prevents rust, it stops the iron from reacting with acidic foods, and it gives visually appealing colour. Technically, the enamel is a vitreous or glass-like coating fused to the iron substrate at very high temperature.

But what does this mean for you—practically? Several things. One: heat distribution and retention. Because cast iron responds slowly, you don't want to rush it; instead, you allow it to warm up gently and then rely on its residual heat to cook evenly. Studies have shown that enameled cast iron provides superior heat retention compared to stainless steel or anodized aluminum cookware—water in a Dutch oven of enameled cast iron cools far more slowly than in a stainless pot. What that means: when you finish cooking and take it off the heat, your food will stay warmer longer—important for dish presentation, for serving from table, and for overall kitchen flow.

Two: non-reactivity. Because of the enamel, your pot does not react with acidic ingredients (tomatoes, wine, lemon). Traditional bare cast iron can impart off-flavours when cooking acidic foods; enamel prevents that. So when you simmer a tomato-based ragù, you're not worrying about metal taste or discoloration of the pot. That opens up your cooking range significantly.

Three: durability and ease of cleaning. The enamel surface is less porous than raw cast iron, does not need seasoning in the same way, and is easier to clean. The "glass-like" coating is smoother, less likely to absorb oils or hold onto flavours. At the same time, because cast iron beneath is heavy and robust, the construction is long-lasting. However—and this is important—you do have to respect the enamel's limitations. Because the coating is glass-like, it can chip or crack if subjected to extreme thermal shock (like pouring cold water into a hot pot) or sharp impact, and metal utensils dragging across it frequently can scratch the finish.

Four: compatibility across heat sources. Cast iron is inductive by nature (because iron is magnetic), so your enameled cast iron Dutch oven works on gas, electric, ceramic and induction cooktops—and in the oven. That versatility means fewer tools in your kitchen, and the ability to go from stovetop to oven to table.

For you, as a user, that means you benefit from best-in-class cookware—but that also comes with the responsibility of understanding how to use it well. Preheating gently, avoiding abrupt temperature changes, using utensils that respect the finish—those are not cosmetic suggestions; they're rooted in material science. When you cook a stew, roast a whole chicken, or bake bread in your Dutch oven, you're working with hundreds of layers of cast iron and enamel, all functioning together to produce flavor, texture and reliability.

In short: your pot isn't just pretty, it's engineered. And knowing that engineering helps you use it smarter, clean it better, and let it serve you for years—decades—of cooking. With that grounding in place, we'll move next into how to inspect, select and prepare your Dutch oven for first use—and then we'll dive deep into techniques, care, and recipes. You're off to a strong start.

CHAPTER 2

ANATOMY OF A DUTCH OVEN

There's something almost architectural about a Dutch oven. Its curves, its weight, the snug way the lid sits down onto the pot—it's a design that looks simple but hides real precision. Many of us buy one for the beauty of that enamel or because we've heard it "does everything," yet when it arrives we realize there's more to understand. How big should it be? Why are some round and others oval? And what about those different handles, knobs, or model names we see online? Before you can cook confidently, it helps to know exactly what you're holding in your hands.

Think of this chapter as the anatomy lesson of your Le Creuset Dutch oven. We'll take a gentle but detailed look inside and out—exploring size, shape, capacity, and the features that make one model slightly different from another. Understanding these elements will help you make better choices, avoid common frustrations, and match the right pot to the right purpose.

As with anything built to last a lifetime, the design choices aren't random. They've evolved from almost a century of feedback between cooks and craftspeople. The handles are shaped for balance when you lift a pot full of stew; the lid's weight controls moisture; the curve at the base prevents food from sticking. Every millimeter has a reason. Once you learn how these parts work together, you'll see your Dutch oven not as a heavy mystery but as a brilliantly engineered partner in the kitchen.

Sizes, Shapes, and Capacities Explained

When you first browse Le Creuset's line, the variety can be surprising. There are tiny one-quart cocottes that could hold a dip or a dessert, mid-sized 5½-quart models that seem to appear in every recipe blog, and grand 9-quart versions large enough for a holiday roast. The color might draw your eye, but size and shape will ultimately define how useful the piece becomes in your daily cooking.

Let's start with capacity, because that's what most buyers wrestle with first. Le Creuset lists its Dutch ovens by quarts or litres, referring to the interior volume from base to rim. A 1- or 2-quart pot is small: perfect for side dishes, sauces, or personal servings. These little pieces often double as bakeware—think individual mac-and-cheese portions or a bubbling fruit crumble. Step up to a 3½- or 4½-quart, and you're in weeknight territory: stews for two to four people, small batches of soup, or a compact loaf of bread. The 5½-quart model, often called the "sweet spot," can handle nearly any recipe for a family of four to six. It's deep enough for soups yet not too heavy to maneuver easily. If you regularly cook for a crowd, 7¼- to 9-quart ovens are generous enough for large roasts, whole chickens, or batches of chili to feed a party.

But volume is only part of the story. The shape—round or oval—changes how the pot behaves on your stove. A round Dutch oven fits neatly over a single burner and spreads heat evenly, making it ideal for soups, risottos, or bread. The oval design, by contrast, gives you space for elongated cuts of meat—racks of lamb, pork loins, or a full chicken lying comfortably without crowding. It's especially handy if you braise or roast often. The trade-off? On smaller stovetops, the ends of an oval pot may sit off-center from the heat source, so rotating the pot occasionally helps maintain even cooking.

Within each form, the proportions—height to width—also influence performance. A wider base provides more surface area for browning meat or reducing sauce; a deeper shape helps with volume and moisture retention. That's why many cooks eventually collect two different sizes or shapes: one wide and shallow for braising and one taller for soups and slow simmering.

Another subtle detail lies in handle design. Modern Le Creuset models feature large, looped handles that can accommodate oven mitts, making it easier to lift a heavy, hot pot. Older or smaller versions sometimes have smaller grips, charming but less forgiving. It's the sort of thing you don't notice until you're removing a pot full of bubbling stew from a 400-degree oven—then it matters. Likewise, the lid knob has evolved: stainless-steel knobs can handle any oven temperature, while classic phenolic knobs (the black resin ones) are heat-safe up to 480 °F. Many owners eventually upgrade knobs for both style and practicality.

Colour deserves a mention, too, though it's more emotional than functional. Le Creuset's enamel palette spans dozens of shades, from the iconic Flame orange to deep Caribbean blues and soft neutrals. While color doesn't change performance, it can influence how you use the piece. Some home cooks prefer lighter interiors because it's easier to monitor browning; others like darker interiors for hiding stains. The glossy outer enamel, beyond beauty, also protects against rust and makes cleanup easier.

Finally, weight—often the biggest surprise to first-time users. A typical 5½-quart Dutch oven weighs around 11 pounds empty. That heft isn't accidental; it's part of what gives cast iron its even heating. But knowing this helps you plan: use two hands, clear a safe landing space, and remember that the pot retains heat long after you remove it from the burner. That thermal inertia is your friend—it keeps food warm for serving—but it also means patience when preheating and cooling.

When you start recognizing these small design choices, you'll see the Dutch oven less as a single object and more as a system. Capacity governs how much food you can make, shape dictates what type of food suits it best, and design details—handles, lid, knob—affect how pleasant it is to use day after day. Understanding this anatomy allows you to buy once, buy smart, and build a lasting relationship with a tool that will quite literally outlive your stovetop.

Signature vs. Classic: What's the Difference?

If you've ever browsed Le Creuset's catalog or stood in a kitchen store comparing models side by side, you've probably noticed two main types of Dutch ovens: the Signature and the Classic (sometimes called "Traditional"). At first glance, they look almost identical — same vibrant enamel, same cast-iron body, same aura of quality. But look closer, and the differences start to reveal themselves in subtle yet meaningful ways. Understanding these distinctions helps you make an informed choice, especially if you're investing in your first Le Creuset or upgrading an older one.

Let's begin with a bit of background. The Classic model is the original — the one that built Le Creuset's reputation through most of the 20th century. It's the version that sat on the stoves of French bistros, in Julia Child's kitchen, and in countless family homes. The Signature line, introduced decades later, was Le Creuset's thoughtful modernization of the original, created in response to home cooks who loved tradition but wanted more comfort and versatility. In essence, the Signature model didn't reinvent the Dutch oven — it refined it.

So, what are those refinements? The first and most noticeable is in the handles. The Classic version's handles are smaller and more delicate, requiring a firm grip and often both hands, especially when you're wearing oven mitts. In contrast, the Signature line features wider, more ergonomic handles, designed to comfortably fit your fingers or a thick mitt. That extra space makes a big difference when maneuvering a hot, heavy pot from stove to oven to table. It's one of those small upgrades that you might not notice until you use it — and then you'll never want to go back.

Next comes the lid design, another subtle evolution. On the Classic model, the lid fits snugly but lightly, creating a fine seal but allowing some steam to escape. The Signature's lid is slightly heavier and more domed, which enhances moisture retention and helps prevent liquid loss during long braises or simmering soups. That's particularly handy for dishes that rely on maintaining consistent humidity inside the pot — think of a slow-cooked boeuf bourguignon or a pot roast that stays melt-in-your-mouth tender.

You'll also find a difference in the lid knob. The older Classic models typically came with a phenolic knob (black resin), which is heat-resistant up to 480 °F — perfectly safe for most baking and roasting tasks. The Signature, however, now ships with a stainless steel knob that can handle any oven temperature without concern. This gives you full freedom for bread baking, high-temperature roasting, and even broiling. Many long-time Le Creuset owners have upgraded their Classic knobs for this reason alone.

Inside the pot, you'll spot another improvement: the interior enamel coating. Both models feature Le Creuset's signature smooth enamel, but the Signature line has a slightly lighter, more durable sand-colored enamel that's designed to resist staining and make it easier to monitor browning. It's not just cosmetic; that pale interior acts like a built-in visual cue, letting you see when butter turns from golden to nutty brown or when onions start to caramelize. The Classic's enamel, by comparison, is sometimes a bit darker and slightly less resistant to scratches over long-term use.

Even the lid markings and branding reflect this evolution. On Signature models, you'll see a bolder, more defined "Le Creuset" embossing and a smoother gradient in the enamel color — a sign of refinements in the glazing process that have improved with technology. The Signature also often has a slightly thicker base for better heat distribution and stability, though both models perform exceptionally well.

Functionally, both cook beautifully — no question there. You'll get the same even heat, the same velvety sauces, the same slow-cooked magic that defines cast iron cooking. The real difference lies in comfort, durability, and versatility. The Signature is simply easier to live with day to day. It's a product of evolution — the same classic soul dressed in smarter details for modern kitchens.

For many cooks, nostalgia plays a role. Some cherish the Classic because it's the pot their mother or grandmother used; others prefer the Signature for its improved ergonomics. If you cook frequently or bake bread regularly, the Signature's wider handles and stainless knob make it a clear winner. But if you're drawn to tradition and want a slightly lighter piece that still performs like a dream, the Classic will never disappoint.

It's worth mentioning, too, that both models are completely compatible with all stovetops — gas, electric, induction, or ceramic — and both can go seamlessly from stovetop to oven to table. So, whether you're simmering soup or baking a boule of crusty artisan bread, you'll get Le Creuset's signature results no matter which one you own.

Choosing between the two isn't really a matter of right or wrong. It's about personality — how you cook, what feels comfortable in your hands, and what story you want your cookware to tell. The Signature represents refinement; the Classic represents heritage. And when you think about it, that balance between past and present is exactly what's made Le Creuset endure for nearly a century.

Choosing the Right Dutch Oven for Your Cooking Style

Buying a Le Creuset Dutch oven isn't just a kitchen purchase — it's more like adopting a lifelong cooking companion. Because of that, it's worth taking a few moments to think beyond size or color and consider your actual cooking style. What do you make most often? Do you gravitate toward slow, cozy meals or quick weeknight dinners? Do you bake bread or prefer hearty soups and stews? The right Dutch oven should match not only your recipes but also your rhythms in the kitchen.

Let's start with one of the biggest factors: how you cook, not just what you cook. If your weeknights are busy and you rely on one-pot meals, a mid-sized round Dutch oven — typically the 5½-quart Signature model — is your best friend. It's the most versatile size, large enough for batch cooking but not so heavy that you dread pulling it from the cupboard. You can sauté onions, brown meat, simmer soup, and bake a loaf of bread all in the same pot. It's the Goldilocks of Dutch ovens — not too big, not too small, just right.

Now, if your cooking style leans toward slow-cooked family meals — braised short ribs, pulled pork, or a big pot of chili — you might prefer a larger capacity, something in the 7¼- to 9-quart range. The extra space prevents crowding, which is key for proper browning and flavor development. Meat sears better when it has room, and sauces reduce more evenly when they're not crammed into the pot. Plus, a large oven gives you the flexibility to cook once and eat twice — ideal for meal preppers or anyone feeding a family.

On the other hand, if your style is precision cooking — think risottos, sauces, or smaller-batch meals — a 3½- or 4½-quart round oven is a dream. It heats faster, uses less oil, and allows for more control. Smaller pots also make wonderful presentation pieces for side dishes or desserts when you're entertaining.

For bread bakers, the Dutch oven has become almost legendary. Its heavy lid traps steam, creating the crisp crust and chewy interior that rival artisan loaves from a bakery. If bread is your passion, a 4½- to 5½-quart round oven is ideal — roomy enough for a full boule but compact enough to hold steam efficiently. Some bakers even keep a dedicated pot just for baking, seasoned by countless loaves over time.

If you're more of a roast or braise enthusiast, an oval Dutch oven might fit your style better. Its elongated shape accommodates long cuts of meat — brisket, pork tenderloin, even a whole chicken. It also fits beautifully in the oven for roasting vegetables or baking casseroles. However, because of its shape, an oval pot may not sit perfectly over a single burner on smaller stoves, so it's often best paired with a wide gas burner or induction cooktop that distributes heat evenly.

Beyond size and shape, think about how often you cook. Daily cooks tend to benefit from lighter, more maneuverable sizes — the ones that can go from the stovetop to the dishwasher without breaking a sweat. If your Dutch oven will live on your counter, aesthetics might also matter more: a color that complements your kitchen and inspires you to cook. After all, Le Creuset is as much a piece of art as it is a tool.

Now, let's talk about versatility versus specialization. A single Dutch oven can handle almost anything, but if you cook across many styles, it might be worth considering more than one. A smaller pot (say, 3½-quart) is perfect for grains, sauces, and sides, while a 7¼-quart handles your weekend stews or sourdough adventures. Many long-time Le Creuset owners build their collection this way — gradually, piece by piece, until they have the perfect tool for every occasion.

You might also consider how you like to serve. One of Le Creuset's quiet superpowers is its beauty on the table. Because the enamel is durable and color-rich, your Dutch oven can go straight from oven to table to fridge. For family-style dining — soups, pasta, braised vegetables — it doubles as serving ware. In that case, choose a color you love seeing in the center of your table.

There's also the question of stovetop type. Gas burners are forgiving and evenly heat most pot shapes, but induction stoves reward flat-bottomed, round designs for maximum contact. Electric coils and glass tops can handle either, though round pots tend to heat more evenly. If your kitchen leans modern with induction or ceramic surfaces, a round Signature model is the safest and most efficient choice.

Another factor is weight and comfort. Cast iron isn't light — that's part of its magic, but it also means you need to feel comfortable lifting it, especially when it's full of hot food. If you struggle with wrist strength or prefer something easier to handle, consider staying under the 6-quart range. The 4½- or 5½-quart model gives you all the performance without the strain. The Signature's wide handles also make a noticeable difference in comfort and control.

If you cook mostly for two people, you might think a small Dutch oven is best, but many experienced cooks recommend going one size up. The reason? Flexibility. Leftovers are easy to store, and recipes designed for 5- or 6-quart pots will fit comfortably without adjustments. It's better to have a bit of breathing room than to crowd your ingredients — and your pot will still perform beautifully at smaller volumes.

Another consideration is storage and frequency of use. A Dutch oven is meant to live in plain sight — on a stovetop, open shelf, or sideboard — not buried in a cabinet. If counter space is limited, think about a size that feels right visually as well as practically. The 5½-quart round model looks balanced and proportionate in most kitchens, while larger sizes can dominate smaller spaces.

Le Creuset also makes specialized shapes — like the brasier, which has lower sides and a wider base for shallow braises and searing, or the French oven, designed for gentler stewing and baking. Some cooks start with a classic Dutch oven, then expand into these shapes as their confidence grows. Each has its own personality and purpose, but all share the same heritage of craftsmanship.

In the end, the best Dutch oven for you is the one that makes you want to cook more often. That might sound sentimental, but it's true. The right size and shape won't just improve your results — they'll make the process itself more joyful. When your pot feels like an extension of your hands, when it responds just as you expect, that's when you know you've chosen well.

If you love to experiment, start with the most adaptable choice — a 5½-quart round Signature Dutch oven. You'll use it for everything from soups to bread to braised chicken. If you already know your favorite type of cooking — baking, braising, or entertaining — tailor your choice accordingly. The beauty of Le Creuset is that there's no wrong answer; every pot is crafted to perform, endure, and inspire.

As you hold one in your hands, you can feel the weight of its history — nearly a century of refinement poured into enamel and iron. Yet it's also personal. Every Dutch oven tells a different story depending on who's cooking with it. Yours might become the pot that simmers winter stews for decades or the one that bakes your first perfect loaf of bread. Choosing the right one is the first step in that journey, and now that you understand its anatomy, you're ready to begin.

CHAPTER 3

BEFORE THE FIRST USE

There's a certain excitement that comes with unboxing a new Le Creuset Dutch oven. The weight of it in your hands, the smoothness of that glossy enamel, and the sense that you've just invested in something that will last a lifetime—it's both thrilling and a little intimidating. You might be tempted to wash it quickly and jump straight into your first stew or loaf of bread, but before you do, it's worth slowing down to get to know your pot. The first use sets the tone for how it performs for years to come.

Even though Le Creuset Dutch ovens are ready to use right out of the box, a little attention and understanding at the start will help you get the best results. Unlike ordinary cookware, enameled cast iron behaves in its own way—it heats differently, retains warmth longer, and responds to temperature changes more deliberately. By learning how to prepare, preheat, and handle it properly from the beginning, you'll avoid common beginner mistakes and build habits that make cooking smoother and more enjoyable.

In this chapter, we'll walk through the essential first steps: how to inspect and prepare your Dutch oven before cooking, the dos and don'ts of preheating (which is where many new users slip up), and what makes the heat retention and distribution of enameled cast iron so special. By the time you finish, you'll understand not just how to use your Le Creuset, but *how it works*—and that's the secret to effortless, confident cooking.

How to Inspect and Prepare Your Dutch Oven

Before your first meal, take a few minutes to give your Dutch oven a careful look. This isn't about finding flaws—it's about familiarizing yourself with the details that make it unique. Every Le Creuset piece is hand-inspected at multiple stages during manufacturing, but a personal once-over ensures everything is in perfect condition and gives you confidence in your new tool.

Start by removing the lid and checking the enamel surface inside and out. The finish should be glossy, smooth, and even in color. Because each pot is individually cast and hand-finished, small variations—like subtle dimples, color gradients, or a faint ring near the rim—are normal and part of its handcrafted charm. What you *shouldn't* see are cracks, chips, or rough spots where the enamel didn't fully bond. If you find a sharp imperfection, contact Le Creuset's customer service before using the pot; they're known for excellent warranty support.

Next, check the rim of both the lid and the pot. The very edge of the rim isn't enameled—it's coated with a durable black protective layer that seals the cast iron beneath. This area is normal and intentional; it helps the lid fit snugly and prevents chipping. Just make sure it's smooth to the touch. Also inspect the lid knob and handles to ensure they're secure. If your model has a stainless-steel knob, it should feel firm with no looseness when you twist it.

Once you're satisfied, give your Dutch oven a gentle wash before its first use. Fill your sink with warm water and a small amount of mild dish soap. Use a soft sponge or cloth—never a scouring pad—to remove any manufacturing residue or dust from packaging. Rinse thoroughly and dry completely with a clean towel. This simple wash removes any residual oils or factory particles and gets your pot ready for cooking.

There's no need to season a Le Creuset Dutch oven the way you would bare cast iron. The enamel coating is already sealed and nonreactive, meaning it won't rust or absorb flavors. However, a light preparation step can help. Before cooking for the first time, rub a few drops of neutral oil (like vegetable or canola) over the inner surface with a paper towel, then wipe it clean. This micro-layer of oil helps condition the enamel and enhances the initial cooking performance, especially during the first few uses.

When drying, resist the temptation to leave it upside down on a towel; instead, set it right side up with the lid off to allow air circulation. This prevents moisture from getting trapped and helps preserve the enamel's luster. Store your Dutch oven with the lid slightly ajar if you're not using it right away—this keeps air flowing and prevents any musty odors from forming inside.

Once your pot is clean, dry, and admired for a few minutes (which every owner does, let's be honest), it's ready to meet the heat. But before you light your burner, it's important to understand how to introduce it properly to temperature—because this is where the difference between good cooking and great cooking begins.

The Dos and Don'ts of Preheating

One of the most common mistakes new Dutch oven owners make is treating it like any other pan. With stainless steel, you can crank up the heat and toss in oil right away. With nonstick, you can preheat quickly on medium. But enameled cast iron is different—it's heavier, thicker, and designed to retain heat, not rush into it. Learning how to preheat your Le Creuset properly will extend its life and give you much better results.

Here's the first golden rule: **never preheat an empty Dutch oven over high heat.** This is probably the single most important thing to remember. Because enameled cast iron distributes heat so evenly, the surface can reach high temperatures faster than you realize. If it's empty, the enamel can overheat and discolor, and oils added afterward may burn instantly. Over time, repeated overheating can even lead to dulling or tiny cracks in the enamel surface.

Instead, always preheat gradually. Place the pot on the burner and start with low or medium-low heat for the first minute or two. Then, after a minute, increase it to medium if your recipe requires it. This gradual process allows the iron core and the enamel coating to warm together, preventing thermal shock.

The next rule: **always add oil or liquid before the pot gets too hot.** You can test readiness the same way you might with stainless steel—add a drop of water and see if it sizzles gently. If it evaporates instantly or jumps off the surface, the pot is already too hot. A good rhythm is to start heating, add your oil within 30–60 seconds, and then allow both to come up to temperature together.

Another tip: choose the right **burner size**. Because Le Creuset Dutch ovens are heavy and wide, a small burner under a large pot can create uneven heating and potentially scorch the enamel in the center. Use the burner that most closely matches the pot's diameter so the heat spreads evenly across the base. On gas stoves, adjust the flame so it doesn't lick up the sides; for induction or electric tops, use moderate settings and give the pot time to warm fully before increasing intensity.

If you're transferring your Dutch oven from stovetop to oven, let it adjust gradually there, too. Avoid moving a cold pot directly into a hot oven. Instead, preheat the oven with the pot inside or let the pot warm up gently before baking. Sudden temperature swings can stress the enamel and cause small hairline cracks, especially around the rim or handles.

It's also worth mentioning that **preheating is not always necessary**. Many recipes—especially soups, stews, and slow braises—begin with cold ingredients and build heat gradually. In those cases, starting cold is actually beneficial, as it lets flavors develop and prevents burning. On the other hand, for browning meat, caramelizing onions, or baking bread, controlled preheating makes all the difference.

For example, if you're searing short ribs, you'll want the oil to shimmer before adding the meat—this means the pot is at the right temperature. But for a loaf of sourdough, you might preheat the empty pot (with its lid) in the oven for 30 minutes so it acts like a mini steam oven when you drop in your dough. These are two opposite uses of preheating, and learning when each applies is part of mastering your Dutch oven.

In summary: go slow, be mindful, and resist the urge to blast the heat. Cast iron rewards patience, and once you understand its rhythm, it becomes second nature. That brings us to another key concept that defines your Dutch oven's magic—its heat retention and distribution.

Understanding Heat Retention and Distribution

If you've ever noticed how food stays warm in a Dutch oven long after the stove is turned off, you've witnessed one of its most remarkable qualities: heat retention. This is the core of why Le Creuset cookware performs so differently from stainless steel or aluminum pans. Beneath that elegant enamel lies cast iron—a metal that doesn't just conduct heat, but holds onto it like a reservoir.

Let's break that down a bit. When you heat your Dutch oven, the thick iron walls absorb and store energy. Instead of letting that energy escape quickly, as thin metals do, it's released slowly and evenly across the cooking surface. That's what gives your stew its gentle simmer and your bread its perfectly crisp crust. The enamel layer on top doesn't interfere with that process; it simply protects the iron and distributes heat smoothly so you don't get hot spots.

The result is incredibly stable temperature control. Once your pot reaches the right heat, it stays there with very little fluctuation. That's why Dutch ovens are ideal for slow-cooked dishes—once you get them simmering, you can reduce the heat to low, cover the lid, and walk away. The pot does the work for you, maintaining an even, steady environment that's hard to achieve with lighter cookware.

But with great power comes a bit of responsibility. Because cast iron retains heat so well, it also takes time to cool down. If you overheat or burn something, the pot won't instantly drop in temperature when you turn off the burner. This is why learning to cook at medium or medium-low settings is key. With practice, you'll find that you rarely need high heat for anything. Even browning meat or searing vegetables can be done beautifully at moderate temperatures in a Le Creuset.

The lid also plays a huge role in heat retention and moisture control. A Dutch oven's lid is heavy and precisely fitted, creating a mini-ecosystem inside your pot. As steam rises from the food, it condenses on the underside of the lid and drips back down, continuously basting your ingredients. This self-moisturizing process keeps meats tender, sauces rich, and flavors concentrated. When you lift the lid after hours of simmering, you're greeted by aromas that feel deeper and more integrated than anything you'd get from a lighter pot.

Another advantage of even heat distribution is how forgiving it makes cooking. If you've ever had food stick or burn in a thin pan, you'll appreciate how a Le Creuset gives you more control. You can sauté onions, deglaze, simmer, and reduce without constantly adjusting the flame. Everything cooks at a calm, predictable pace. It's also why these pots excel for baking—when preheated, the entire interior becomes a consistent oven chamber, perfect for artisan bread or baked pasta.

Understanding this characteristic helps you adapt your recipes. You might find that soups need less stirring, sauces need less reduction, and stews taste richer with the same ingredients. The pot simply manages heat better than most cookware, allowing flavors to meld without scorching or drying out.

One final point about heat: your Dutch oven's enamel coating means it reacts more gently to changes in temperature compared to bare cast iron. This makes it safe for acidic foods like tomato sauce or wine reductions—things that would strip seasoning from uncoated iron. However, it also means you should still treat it with care: avoid adding cold liquids to a very hot pot or vice versa. Always let it adjust naturally.

Once you understand how heat moves and behaves inside your Dutch oven, cooking becomes almost intuitive. You'll learn to trust that you don't need to rush; you can turn the burner down, walk away, and return to a meal that's cooked perfectly from edge to center. That's the quiet magic of Le Creuset—patience rewarded with flavor.

CHAPTER 4

MASTERING THE BASICS

Every cook remembers the moment they stop following recipes word-for-word and start *feeling* their way through a dish — sensing when to stir, when to lower the heat, and when to let something rest just a little longer. That instinct doesn't happen overnight. It's built through time, through observation, and most importantly, through understanding your tools. And when your tool happens to be a Le Creuset Dutch oven, mastering the basics becomes not only achievable but truly enjoyable.

The Dutch oven is as versatile as it is beautiful. You can sear a roast, braise short ribs, bake crusty bread, or simmer a velvety soup all in the same pot. Its design—heavy enamel-coated cast iron with a perfectly fitted lid—creates an environment that's both forgiving and consistent. But to unlock that full potential, you need to know how to handle it properly. The difference between a decent result and a "how did I make this at home?" level of deliciousness often comes down to mastering a few foundational techniques.

This chapter will guide you through those essential cooking methods: searing, braising, baking, and roasting. Then we'll look at the best ways to transition between stovetop and oven, since the Le Creuset is designed for both. Finally, we'll dig into temperature control—arguably the single most important factor in perfect results. With a little patience and an understanding of how your pot behaves, you'll soon be cooking like someone who's owned it for years.

How to Sear, Braise, Bake, and Roast

Let's start with searing, one of the most satisfying things you can do in a Dutch oven. There's something deeply rewarding about the sound of meat hitting hot enamel and the aroma that follows. But searing is more than just browning—it's the foundation of flavor. When you sear correctly, you create what's known as the Maillard reaction: a complex series of chemical changes that turn simple proteins into hundreds of flavor compounds. It's what gives a steak its crust, or stew meat its rich, deep taste.

The key to perfect searing in your Le Creuset is patience. Start by drying your meat thoroughly with paper towels; moisture is the enemy of a good crust. Next, heat a small amount of oil (enough to coat the bottom of the pot) over medium heat until it shimmers. Don't rush this step. If the oil starts smoking heavily, it's too hot—cast iron retains heat so well that you'll scorch the enamel and risk bitterness in your food. Once the oil is ready, add your meat in a single layer, leaving space between pieces. Crowding the pot traps steam, which prevents browning.

Now, resist the urge to move the meat around. Let it sit untouched for a few minutes until a crust naturally forms. You'll know it's ready to turn when it releases easily from the surface. If it sticks, it's not ready yet. Once you flip and sear the other side, you'll notice a golden-brown layer of flavor developing at the bottom of the pot. That's called "fond," and it's pure culinary gold. When you later deglaze the pot with wine, stock, or even a bit of water, those caramelized bits dissolve into your sauce, deepening its flavor immeasurably.

Once searing is done, you've laid the groundwork for another beloved Dutch oven technique: braising. Braising is where the Dutch oven truly shines—it's a slow, gentle cooking process that transforms tough cuts of meat into tender, flavorful masterpieces. Think of short ribs that fall off the bone, coq au vin that tastes like it simmered all day, or pulled pork that practically melts at the touch of a fork.

To braise, you start much like you did with searing—browning your meat and sautéing aromatics like onions, garlic, or carrots in the same pot. Then comes the magic moment: adding liquid. This can be broth, wine, beer, or even coconut milk, depending on the recipe. You don't need to fully submerge the meat; halfway up the sides is perfect. Cover the pot with its heavy lid, which traps steam and moisture, then let time and low heat do the rest. The lid's tight seal helps circulate moisture inside, basting your food continuously as it cooks.

The beauty of braising in a Le Creuset is that you can start on the stovetop and finish in the oven without changing pots. The even heat of the cast iron ensures everything cooks uniformly—no burned edges, no raw centers. Set your oven low (around 300°F to 325°F) and check occasionally to make sure there's still enough liquid. After a few hours, you'll lift the lid to find a dish that's rich, tender, and aromatic, with layers of flavor that taste like you worked twice as hard as you did.

Now let's talk about baking. Many people are surprised to learn that their Dutch oven doubles as an excellent baking vessel. The heavy lid and thick walls mimic a professional bread oven, trapping steam that's essential for a beautiful crust. To bake bread, preheat both the pot and lid in the oven for about 30 minutes before adding your dough. The intense heat of the pot's interior helps the bread rise rapidly (a process called "oven spring"), while the steam keeps the crust crisp and golden. After baking covered for most of the time, remove the lid to let the crust finish browning.

Beyond bread, the Dutch oven is wonderful for cobblers, casseroles, and even desserts like fruit crisps. Because of its even heat distribution, baked dishes cook uniformly without hot spots. You can also roast meats or vegetables in it. Roasting in a Dutch oven is slightly different from baking in a pan because the pot traps more heat and moisture. For meats, this means juicier results with less risk of drying out. For vegetables, it means caramelized edges and soft, flavorful interiors.

To roast successfully, preheat the oven and consider using a small rack or layer of vegetables (like carrots or onions) to elevate your meat slightly. This allows air and heat to circulate evenly. A quick sear before roasting helps develop flavor, while the closed lid ensures your roast stays moist. Toward the end of cooking, remove the lid to let the top brown beautifully.

In short, your Le Creuset isn't just a pot—it's a multi-tool that can replace several pieces of cookware. Once you master these core methods, you'll find yourself using it for nearly everything, from weekday dinners to special-occasion feasts.

Proper Techniques for Stovetop and Oven Cooking

Switching between stovetop and oven cooking is one of the most powerful advantages of using a Le Creuset Dutch oven. It allows you to build layers of flavor in a single pot, minimizing cleanup and maximizing efficiency. But there are a few techniques that can make this process smoother and safer.

On the stovetop, it's all about heat control and stability. Because cast iron retains heat, it doesn't respond instantly when you adjust the flame. If you notice your food starting to brown too quickly, lower the heat immediately—it might take a few minutes for the change to take effect, but it will stabilize beautifully once it does. Always use medium or medium-low settings unless a recipe specifically calls for high heat. Remember, with enameled cast iron, gentle and steady wins every time.

When sautéing vegetables or browning meat, use oils with a high smoke point, like canola, grapeseed, or avocado oil. Avoid butter or olive oil for high-temperature tasks, as they burn more easily and can leave sticky residue on the enamel. If you want to add butter for flavor, do it later in the cooking process.

If your recipe requires a long simmer—like a stew or chili—bring the pot to a boil first, then reduce it to low. Once the contents start to bubble gently, cover it and let the Dutch oven work its magic. You'll notice that even on low heat, it maintains a steady simmer without much effort. That's the beauty of its thick, heavy construction: it acts like a thermal battery, storing and releasing energy gradually.

When moving from stovetop to oven, make sure your pot and its contents are ready for the change. Sudden temperature shocks can harm the enamel, so never transfer a cold Dutch oven into a blazing-hot oven or vice versa. If you're baking or braising, preheat the oven with the pot inside or allow it to adjust gradually to avoid stress cracks.

The lid deserves special mention here. It's not just decorative—it's an essential part of the cooking system. When used on the stovetop, it helps regulate evaporation and retain moisture. In the oven, it creates a sealed environment that turns your Dutch oven into a mini convection chamber. If you want a dish with a crisp top or reduced sauce, leave the lid slightly ajar toward the end of cooking to allow steam to escape.

After removing your pot from the oven, always place it on a heat-resistant surface, not a cold countertop or wet towel. The sudden change in temperature could cause the enamel to craze (tiny hairline cracks that appear on the surface). A trivet, wooden board, or folded kitchen towel works perfectly.

Finally, be mindful of the handles. The entire pot, including the knob, gets extremely hot. Even if the stainless-steel knob is oven-safe, it holds heat like the rest of the pot. Always use thick, dry oven mitts or silicone grips when handling. You'll quickly get into the habit of treating it with the same respect you'd give a blazing campfire—it's your friend, but it demands care.

The more you cook this way—starting on the stovetop, finishing in the oven—the more intuitive it becomes. You'll begin to see how flavors evolve differently in each environment: the stovetop builds intensity through browning, while the oven softens and melds everything together. It's a dance between direct heat and gentle enclosure, and your Le Creuset is the perfect partner.

Temperature Control Tips for Perfect Results

If there's one secret that separates average Dutch oven meals from extraordinary ones, it's temperature control. Understanding how heat behaves in your Le Creuset is the single most valuable skill you can develop.

First, remember this rule of thumb: with enameled cast iron, **low and slow almost always beats high and fast.** Because the pot holds and distributes heat so evenly, it's rare that you'll ever need high heat. In fact, most recipes that call for "medium-high" can be done perfectly at medium in your Le Creuset.

When searing, medium or medium-high is plenty. The enamel will reach optimal browning temperature quickly, and the heat will stay consistent. If you're simmering soups or sauces, low is your best friend. The goal is gentle movement—small bubbles that break the surface occasionally, not a rolling boil. A gentle simmer prevents food from sticking, scorching, or drying out.

In the oven, temperatures between 275°F and 350°F cover most cooking needs. The lower end is perfect for slow-cooked braises, while the higher end works for roasting and baking. Because of the pot's excellent heat retention, you can even reduce oven temperatures by about 25°F from what you'd use in a regular pan and still get great results.

Keep in mind that the Dutch oven's thick walls mean it takes time to change temperature. If you overheat the pot, it won't cool down instantly when you lower the flame. It's better to start with a moderate temperature and adjust upward if needed. Over time, you'll develop a feel for it—your pot will almost "teach" you how it likes to be treated.

Moisture control is also part of temperature control. A tightly sealed lid traps steam, which keeps dishes juicy but can also slow down thickening. If your sauce or stew looks too thin, remove the lid for the last 15–20 minutes of cooking to let some liquid evaporate. Conversely, if things are drying out too quickly, add a splash of broth or water and re-cover.

For baking, particularly bread, internal temperature is key. If you're serious about consistency, consider using an instant-read thermometer. Most artisan loaves are done when they reach 200–210°F in the center. Removing the lid midway through baking helps develop that beautiful, crisp crust we associate with bakery-style bread.

Lastly, remember that residual heat continues to cook food even after the pot is off the burner. When you turn off the heat, let your dish rest for a few minutes before serving. The flavors will settle, and the texture will improve. This carryover cooking is especially useful for rice dishes, braised meats, or baked casseroles that need a moment to "come together."

Once you've mastered temperature and timing, you'll discover that your Le Creuset rewards mindfulness with reliability. It's a pot that thrives on calm, deliberate cooking. It encourages you to slow down, taste as you go, and trust the process—a refreshing contrast to the rush of modern kitchen gadgets.

CHAPTER 5

EVERYDAY COOKING TECHNIQUES

There's a moment in every cook's journey when the Dutch oven stops being a beautiful piece of cookware sitting on the counter and becomes something much more: a reliable partner in daily cooking. The more you use it, the more you realize it's not just for special meals or long Sunday braises — it's for everything. Breakfast oatmeal, weeknight soups, pasta sauces, baked breads, even desserts. Once you learn its rhythm, it becomes the pot you reach for instinctively, no matter what's on the menu.

The Le Creuset Dutch oven is built for *everyday ease*. Its cast iron core and smooth enamel coating make it remarkably forgiving — it holds steady heat, cleans easily, and transitions seamlessly from stovetop to oven to table. But to make it part of your daily cooking flow, it helps to understand a few core techniques that fit naturally into busy lives. That's what this chapter is about: bringing out the best of your pot, every single day, without fuss or intimidation.

We'll start with slow cooking — one of the simplest, most satisfying ways to use your Dutch oven. Then we'll move to soups, stews, and sauces, where the pot's heat retention truly shines. We'll talk about one-pot meals (your new best friend on weeknights when you're short on time) and finally, we'll explore the magic of baking bread — the part where your Le Creuset transforms from a humble pot into a mini artisan bakery.

By the end of this chapter, you'll have a practical understanding of how to use your Dutch oven for real life — not just perfect Instagram-worthy meals, but the comforting, dependable dishes that make home cooking feel effortless.

Slow Cooking Made Simple

There's something deeply comforting about slow cooking — the kind of cooking that fills your home with a steady, mouthwatering aroma that builds all afternoon.

The beauty of a Le Creuset Dutch oven is that it turns slow cooking into an art form without needing fancy appliances. You don't need a separate slow cooker or pressure cooker; your pot can do it all, with more flavor and control.

At its heart, slow cooking is about two things: gentle heat and time. The enameled cast iron of your Le Creuset is designed to deliver both. Because it retains heat so evenly, it creates a steady, consistent temperature that's perfect for breaking down tough cuts of meat, softening vegetables, and melding flavors into something rich and comforting.

To start, choose your ingredients wisely. Slow cooking works best with cuts that have a bit of fat and connective tissue — things like chuck roast, short ribs, pork shoulder, or chicken thighs. These cuts transform into tender, flavorful bites when cooked low and slow. Leaner meats, on the other hand, can dry out with extended cooking.

Begin by building a flavor base. Heat a small amount of oil in the Dutch oven and brown your meat on all sides. Don't skip this step — it's what gives your dish depth and body. Once browned, remove the meat and sauté aromatics like onions, garlic, and carrots. Add spices or herbs next; letting them bloom in the hot oil for a minute brings out their full fragrance.

Then add your cooking liquid — broth, wine, tomatoes, or even coconut milk, depending on the recipe. Return the meat to the pot, making sure the liquid comes at least halfway up the sides. Bring it to a gentle simmer on the stovetop, then cover with the lid and transfer to a preheated oven set between 275°F and 325°F. From there, time does the work.

The key is patience. Most slow-cooked dishes take two to four hours, depending on size and cut. You'll know it's ready when the meat yields easily to a fork and the sauce has thickened into something velvety and full of flavor.

The Dutch oven's design makes this process nearly foolproof. Its heavy lid locks in moisture, so you don't have to worry about your food drying out. Unlike an electric slow cooker, which heats from the bottom and can create uneven spots, your Dutch oven distributes heat uniformly through every inch. The result? More flavor, better texture, and a hands-off process that fits beautifully into your day.

And the best part? Clean-up is a breeze. When you're done, you'll find that most of what's left simply lifts away with warm water and a soft sponge — no soaking overnight, no scrubbing for hours.

How to Make Soups, Stews, and Sauces

If the Dutch oven has a love language, it's soup. Whether you're making a quick weeknight tomato soup or an all-day beef stew, this pot makes it easy to create food that feels like a hug in a bowl.

The secret to great soups and stews lies in layering flavor, and your Le Creuset is perfectly suited for that. You start by sautéing your aromatics — onions, celery, garlic, carrots — right in the pot. Because the enamel surface holds heat evenly, you can sweat them gently without burning or scorching. Once they're soft and fragrant, add your spices or herbs. Toasting them briefly releases their essential oils and deepens the base flavor.

Next, deglaze. This is one of the most satisfying moments in Dutch oven cooking. After sautéing or browning, you'll notice a film of browned bits at the bottom — the fond. Add a splash of liquid, like wine or broth, and use a wooden spoon to scrape those bits loose. They'll dissolve into the liquid, infusing your soup or stew with an incredible depth of flavor that no bouillon cube can replicate.

From there, add your main ingredients — beans, vegetables, grains, or meat — and pour in enough liquid to cover. The heavy lid will trap moisture, allowing the ingredients to simmer gently without constant stirring.

Soups and stews love time, but they don't always need a whole afternoon. Quick soups like lentil or vegetable can be ready in under an hour, while stews or chowders may take a bit longer. Either way, the Dutch oven gives you steady, predictable results. Nothing sticks, nothing burns, and the heat remains consistent.

Sauces, too, benefit from this consistency. Tomato sauces, in particular, can develop beautifully in a Dutch oven. Start with a bit of olive oil and garlic, add your tomatoes, herbs, and a touch of sugar to balance acidity, and let it bubble gently on low heat. Because the pot retains warmth even at low temperatures, the sauce thickens slowly and evenly, developing that rich, home-cooked flavor you just can't rush.

Cream-based sauces work well, too, though you'll want to use gentle heat to avoid curdling. A classic béchamel or cheese sauce, for example, comes together beautifully in a smaller Dutch oven. Stir slowly and consistently, and you'll be rewarded with silky smooth results.

The versatility of your Le Creuset means you can make everything from rustic soups to sophisticated reductions in one pot. It doesn't discriminate between simple comfort food and elegant cooking — it just makes both better.

One-Pot Meals for Busy Days

We all have those days when cooking feels like one more thing on an already full list. You want something wholesome and satisfying, but you don't want to juggle multiple pans or spend an hour cleaning up afterward. That's where one-pot meals come in — and your Dutch oven is the ultimate one-pot meal champion.

The concept is simple: everything cooks in one vessel, from start to finish. That means you can layer flavors, control textures, and still end up with a dish that feels cohesive and comforting.

Start with something like a chicken and rice bake. Sear the chicken thighs first to get a golden crust, then remove them and sauté onions, garlic, and spices in the same pot. Add rice and broth, return the chicken to nestle on top, cover, and bake. In about 30 minutes, you'll have tender, juicy chicken and perfectly cooked rice that's absorbed all the flavors.

Or try pasta dishes — yes, you can make pasta entirely in your Dutch oven. Sauté your aromatics, add uncooked pasta, sauce ingredients, and enough liquid to cook the pasta directly in the sauce. The starch from the noodles thickens the sauce naturally, giving it that restaurant-quality texture without needing a separate pan or colander.

Vegetarian one-pot meals work beautifully, too. Consider lentil curry, vegetable tagine, or a simple ratatouille. Because of the even heat and moisture control, vegetables cook through without becoming mushy, and spices bloom into their fullest flavors.

And here's a tip for maximizing your Dutch oven on busy nights: make more than you need. These meals reheat beautifully, often tasting even better the next day as the flavors continue to meld. The enamel surface also makes storing leftovers safe — once cooled, you can put the entire pot in the fridge.

For truly time-crunched evenings, try pre-prepping ingredients in the morning — chop vegetables, marinate proteins, or measure spices. Then, when dinnertime comes, everything's ready to toss into the pot. The cooking itself is largely hands-off, leaving you time to unwind while dinner simmers away.

A one-pot meal isn't just about convenience; it's about rediscovering the joy of simplicity. With your Le Creuset, even the most modest ingredients can turn into something extraordinary when given the right environment to cook together.

Baking Bread in Your Dutch Oven

There's a certain magic to baking bread in a Dutch oven — a ritual that transforms your kitchen into a bakery and fills your home with the warm, comforting scent of fresh bread. And if you've ever wondered how professional bakers achieve that crisp crust and chewy, airy interior, the secret is simple: steam. Your Le Creuset creates the perfect steamy microclimate for bread to rise and bake beautifully.

The process is easier than most people think. You don't need a professional oven or complicated setup. All you need is your pot, a bit of patience, and a good dough.

Start with a basic no-knead recipe — flour, water, yeast, salt, and time. After mixing and letting it rise (usually overnight for the best flavor), preheat your oven with the Dutch oven inside. Heating both pot and lid ensures that when the dough hits the surface, it gets an instant burst of heat that helps it rise rapidly — bakers call this "oven spring."

Once preheated, carefully transfer your dough onto parchment paper and lower it into the pot. Cover with the lid and bake for the first 20–30 minutes. The enclosed space traps steam from the dough, keeping the crust soft while the inside expands. After that, remove the lid and continue baking until the crust turns deep golden brown.

The result? A loaf that crackles when you tap it, with a beautiful open crumb and a texture that rivals bakery bread.

Beyond traditional loaves, your Dutch oven can handle other baked goods, too — focaccia, dinner rolls, even cobblers and crisps. The even heat ensures perfect caramelization without burning.

One of the most rewarding things about baking in a Le Creuset is how forgiving it is. Even if your dough shaping isn't perfect or your timing is a little off, the pot's steady heat and moisture control tend to balance everything out. It's almost as if the pot *wants* you to succeed.

And here's the best part: once you've done it once, you'll never go back to store-bought bread. There's something deeply satisfying about pulling a hot, golden loaf from the oven, knowing it came from your own hands and your own trusted pot.

CHAPTER 6

ADVANCED COOKING TIPS

There's a special kind of joy that comes when cooking starts to feel natural — when you're no longer worrying about measurements or second-guessing every move, but instead cooking by instinct. It's when you begin to trust your senses — the sound of onions sizzling, the smell of browned butter, the feel of heat under your fingertips. By this stage, your Le Creuset Dutch oven has probably become a familiar and beloved part of your kitchen. You've mastered the basics — searing, simmering, baking, and braising — and now, you're ready to explore the finer details that separate good cooking from great cooking.

This is where things get interesting. Advanced techniques aren't about complexity for its own sake. They're about understanding how to *build flavor*, how to coax out depth from simple ingredients, and how to use your Dutch oven's design to your advantage. A Le Creuset is more than a pot; it's a finely tuned cooking instrument capable of professional results if you know how to handle it.

In this chapter, we'll explore three essential skills that will take your Dutch oven cooking to the next level: **layering flavors, deglazing like a chef, and using your Dutch oven for frying, poaching, and simmering**. These aren't just tricks — they're foundational techniques used by chefs worldwide to create food that feels both refined and soulful. Once you learn them, you'll find that your cooking naturally evolves, becoming richer, more nuanced, and deeply satisfying.

The goal here isn't perfection; it's understanding. Each of these skills builds upon what you already know, helping you cook with confidence and intuition. Whether you're elevating a simple stew, turning out restaurant-quality sauces, or frying chicken with golden crisp perfection, these techniques will help you get the most out of your Dutch oven — and yourself as a cook.

Layering Flavors for Depth

If you've ever wondered why restaurant dishes seem to have that extra something — that depth that makes every bite taste complex and complete — it almost always comes down to one thing: flavor layering. In simple terms, layering flavors means building taste gradually, step by step, instead of tossing everything into the pot at once. It's about patience and attention to detail, and your Le Creuset Dutch oven is perfectly designed for this kind of thoughtful cooking.

Every dish begins with a foundation, and in most cases, that foundation is aromatics. Onions, garlic, leeks, celery, and carrots are the usual suspects. Sautéing them slowly in a bit of fat — olive oil, butter, or rendered bacon — allows their natural sugars to caramelize gently. This is your first layer. Don't rush it. A few extra minutes here can completely transform your final dish.

Once your base is soft and golden, it's time for the next layer: spices and herbs. Toasting them in the warm oil before adding liquid releases essential oils and deepens their fragrance. You'll notice how your kitchen suddenly fills with a richer, more robust aroma — that's the flavor expanding. Dried spices like cumin, paprika, or curry powder love this stage. Fresh herbs, on the other hand, are best saved for the end, when they can add a bright, fresh note to balance the richness.

Next, consider your proteins and vegetables. Searing meat before simmering adds another dimension of flavor through the Maillard reaction — the scientific term for browning that creates those deeply savory notes. The enameled surface of your Le Creuset makes it easy to get an even, golden crust without burning. Don't crowd the pot; give each piece space to brown properly. This browning, these tiny golden bits, are where much of your dish's final character will come from.

Liquids are the next layer — whether it's wine, stock, tomato sauce, or even coconut milk. Each one brings its own personality to the dish. Wine adds acidity and depth; broth builds richness; tomatoes add tang and sweetness. As these liquids mingle with the browned bits on the bottom of your pot, they form the foundation for your sauce or broth — and this is where layering transforms from simple cooking into art.

Finally, seasoning. Salt, pepper, acids like lemon juice or vinegar, and finishing touches like a drizzle of olive oil or a knob of butter can make or break a dish. Add them thoughtfully and at multiple stages. A pinch of salt early helps draw out moisture and balance flavors; a final sprinkle right before serving heightens everything. The same goes for acid — a splash at the end can brighten a heavy stew or make a sauce sing.

What's beautiful about layering flavors in a Dutch oven is how naturally it happens. The pot's heat retention ensures each stage builds evenly without scorching or cooling too quickly. It gives you the time and control to coax flavors instead of forcing them.

Once you start cooking this way — tasting as you go, adjusting, building — you'll never want to return to "dump and stir" recipes again. Layering is how you make simple food taste extraordinary.

Deglazing Like a Chef

If flavor layering is about patience, deglazing is about precision — it's the moment where all your earlier effort pays off in concentrated taste. To deglaze means to add liquid to a hot pan to loosen and dissolve the flavorful browned bits (fond) stuck to the bottom. It's a small act, but it's one that can completely transform a dish from ordinary to unforgettable.

Your Le Creuset Dutch oven is practically built for deglazing. Its smooth enamel surface allows fond to form beautifully as you brown meat or vegetables, but it also releases those bits easily when liquid is added. This dual quality — browning without sticking — is what makes the Dutch oven the professional cook's dream.

Here's how to do it right. After browning meat or sautéing aromatics, you'll notice the fond at the bottom — that golden-brown layer that looks like it might burn if you're not careful. Don't scrape it yet. Instead, remove any larger pieces of food, then pour in your deglazing liquid.

The liquid can be wine, broth, beer, vinegar, or even water, depending on your recipe. The key is to use enough to cover the bottom of the pot — usually about half a cup to one cup. As soon as the liquid hits the hot surface, it sizzles and releases a burst of steam. Use a wooden spoon or silicone spatula to gently scrape the bottom, loosening all that flavorful residue. Within seconds, your liquid will turn darker and more aromatic — that's pure flavor coming to life.

For wine-based dishes, let the liquid simmer for a minute or two to cook off the alcohol. For broths or vinegar, this quick simmer helps reduce and concentrate the flavor. What you're left with is the beginning of a sauce, stew base, or braising liquid that carries layers of complexity.

In French cooking, this step is non-negotiable — it's the foundation of pan sauces, gravies, and braises. But it's not just for fancy meals. Deglazing can elevate a weeknight stir-fry, pasta sauce, or soup. Imagine you've sautéed onions and garlic for a pasta dish — a quick splash of white wine to deglaze before adding tomatoes will add incredible depth and richness.

One of the advantages of deglazing in a Le Creuset is control. The even heat means your fond develops uniformly, without bitter burned spots. The enamel surface makes it easy to see exactly what's happening, and you can scrape confidently without worrying about damaging the pot.

A few tips:

- Always deglaze while the pot is still hot but not scorching.

- Avoid adding cold liquid straight from the fridge; let it come to room temperature to prevent shocking the enamel.

- Choose your liquid wisely — acidic liquids like wine or vinegar add brightness, while broths or cream-based liquids add richness.

Mastering deglazing gives you access to the heart of professional cooking. It's the moment where chemistry and intuition meet — where you transform simple browned bits into a sauce that makes people close their eyes with that first bite and say, "Wow."

Using Your Dutch Oven for Frying, Poaching, and Simmering

One of the most underrated features of a Le Creuset Dutch oven is its versatility with different cooking methods. Most people know it for baking or braising, but few realize how exceptional it is for frying, poaching, and simmering — three techniques that rely heavily on precise temperature control and even heat distribution.

Let's start with frying. The heavy cast iron base of your Dutch oven makes it one of the safest and most effective vessels for deep or shallow frying. Because it retains heat so well, oil temperature stays stable even after adding food, which means crispier, less greasy results. Whether you're frying chicken, doughnuts, or vegetables, consistency is everything — and your pot delivers.

To fry, fill the pot with oil to about one-third full (never more than halfway). Heat the oil slowly over medium heat, using a thermometer if you have one. Ideal frying temperatures range between 325°F and 375°F. When you add food, do it in small batches to prevent the oil from cooling too quickly. The enamel interior ensures that food browns evenly without sticking or scorching, and cleanup afterward is far easier than with traditional steel pots.

Next comes poaching — a gentler, more refined method of cooking where food is submerged in barely simmering liquid, usually between 160°F and 180°F. The Dutch oven's ability to maintain stable low heat makes it perfect for poaching delicate foods like eggs, fish, chicken breasts, or fruit. The key is control: too much heat, and you're boiling; too little, and you're just soaking.

For example, when poaching salmon, a simple mixture of water, white wine, herbs, and lemon slices works beautifully. Bring the liquid to a gentle simmer, then lower the heat and slide the fish in. The goal is for tiny bubbles to rise occasionally — not a rolling boil. Within minutes, you'll have tender, silky fish infused with subtle flavor.

Finally, simmering — perhaps the most common and yet misunderstood technique. Simmering isn't boiling. It's the quiet, steady bubble that coaxes ingredients to blend without breaking them apart. Your Dutch oven's thick walls and tight-fitting lid create the ideal environment for this. Whether you're making chili, curry, or tomato sauce, simmering allows flavors to marry while preventing evaporation.

The lid plays an important role here: keeping it partially open helps reduce and thicken sauces; keeping it closed retains moisture for soups and stews. The even heat means you don't need to stir constantly — just an occasional check to ensure nothing's sticking.

One beautiful advantage of using a Le Creuset for these methods is consistency. You don't have to worry about hotspots or sudden spikes in temperature. Once you find your rhythm, the pot almost seems to regulate itself.

And because it transitions seamlessly from stovetop to oven, you can start frying or simmering and finish cooking in the oven if needed — for instance, crisping up fried chicken or thickening a sauce gently.

Afterward, cleaning is straightforward. Allow the pot to cool, pour out the oil or liquid, and wash with warm, soapy water. The enamel resists staining and doesn't retain odors, so you can go from frying fish one day to baking bread the next without lingering scents.

What's most rewarding about mastering these techniques in your Dutch oven is how they expand your cooking confidence. You'll start to see your pot not just as a single-purpose tool, but as a flexible, responsive partner that can handle nearly any task.

CHAPTER 7

CLEANING YOUR LE CREUSET

There's a quiet moment that comes after cooking a great meal — when the plates are empty, the kitchen smells like garlic and herbs, and your beautiful Le Creuset Dutch oven sits on the stovetop, still radiating warmth. It's been the centerpiece of dinner, the vessel that made everything come together. But now comes the part that every cook faces: cleanup.

For many people, this stage brings a mix of pride and hesitation. You admire how good your pot looks, but you also notice the browned edges, the bits of sauce baked onto the enamel, or perhaps a few dark stains from a hearty stew. You might wonder, "How do I clean this without damaging it?" The good news is, Le Creuset is built to be used — and with the right care, it can stay as stunning as the day you bought it for decades.

Cleaning a Le Creuset Dutch oven isn't complicated, but it does require knowing the right techniques and avoiding the wrong ones. This chapter will guide you through everything from daily cleaning routines to deep-cleaning stubborn stains, understanding what never to do, and how to revive your pot's glossy enamel finish if it starts to look dull. Think of it as learning the art of maintenance — simple rituals that keep your Dutch oven performing beautifully and looking like new.

The truth is, every bit of care you put into cleaning pays off later in performance. A well-maintained enamel surface means better heat distribution, easier cooking, and a pot that always feels inviting to use. So, let's get into it — the practical, foolproof methods that will help you care for your Le Creuset the way it was meant to be cared for.

Daily Cleaning Steps

The best cleaning begins before your meal is even served. When you finish cooking, don't immediately plunge your hot Dutch oven into water — that's the first rule. Instead, let it cool naturally for at least 15–20 minutes. The enamel coating and cast iron expand when hot, and sudden temperature changes (like cold water hitting a hot surface) can cause thermal shock, which may weaken or crack the enamel over time.

Once your pot has cooled, start with warm water and a mild dish soap. Avoid anything harsh or gritty — no abrasive powders or steel wool. A soft sponge, nylon brush, or non-scratch scrubber is all you need for daily cleaning. Le Creuset's enamel is designed to release food easily, so you'll often find that even sticky sauces or bits of food come off with minimal effort once soaked briefly in warm, soapy water.

If you've cooked something particularly rich or oily, fill the pot with warm water and let it soak for 10 to 15 minutes before scrubbing. Most residue will lift right off. For tougher bits, a gentle circular motion with a non-abrasive sponge usually does the trick. Never feel the need to scrub aggressively — patience and warm water work better than force.

After washing, rinse thoroughly with warm water and dry completely with a soft towel. Don't let water sit in the pot or on the rim for too long, as it can cause mineral spots or leave streaks. If you live in an area with hard water, a quick rinse of distilled or filtered water at the end can help keep your enamel bright and spot-free.

For the exterior, especially if you have a colored enamel finish, a simple wipe with warm soapy water is often enough. If grease splatters or baked-on spots appear near the handles or lid, soak them briefly and clean them with a soft brush. Avoid harsh degreasers — they're unnecessary and can dull the enamel's gloss.

Finally, remember the lid. The underside, especially the rim, often collects steam residue or sauce splatters. Wash it with the same care as the pot, paying attention to the edge where it sits on the base. Then dry it fully before storing to prevent moisture buildup, which could lead to dulling or small mineral spots over time.

This simple daily routine — soak, scrub gently, rinse, and dry — is all it takes to keep your Dutch oven looking pristine day after day. The key is consistency. A few mindful minutes after each use prevent long-term buildup and keep your cookware as dependable as the day you brought it home.

Removing Stains and Burnt Residue

Even the most careful cook occasionally ends up with stubborn stains or burnt-on food at the bottom of the pot. Maybe you got distracted while sautéing onions, or perhaps a thick sauce simmered a little too long. It happens to everyone. The trick is not to panic — and definitely not to reach for anything abrasive. Your Le Creuset can handle the job with a few smart techniques and a bit of patience.

Start with the simplest solution: **a warm soak**. Fill the pot with hot (not boiling) water and a few drops of mild dish soap. Let it sit for an hour or even overnight, depending on how stubborn the residue is. Often, that alone softens and loosens most of the burnt-on material, which you can then remove with a non-scratch sponge or nylon brush.

If the stain remains, it's time for the next level: **the baking soda method.** Drain the pot, sprinkle a generous layer of baking soda over the affected area, and add enough warm water to make a paste. Let it sit for 15–30 minutes, then gently scrub in small circles. Baking soda acts as a mild abrasive and natural deodorizer without harming the enamel surface.

For really tough, dark discoloration, try a **boil-cleaning technique**. Fill the pot about halfway with water and add two to three tablespoons of baking soda. Bring it to a gentle simmer on the stove, then turn off the heat and let it cool. As it cools, you'll notice the residue loosening or floating up. Afterward, rinse and wash as usual.

If stains persist after multiple attempts, you can also use a small amount of **Le Creuset's specialized cookware cleaner**, which is designed to polish enamel surfaces safely. It removes stains, restores gloss, and helps bring back the pot's original luster. Always follow the manufacturer's directions and rinse thoroughly afterward.

Avoid using bleach or harsh chemical cleaners, as they can damage the enamel and dull its color. Similarly, stay away from metal scrapers or scouring pads — they can leave fine scratches that make future cleaning harder.

One of the most important things to remember is that minor discoloration, especially inside the pot, is a normal part of the Dutch oven's life. Over time, light staining can develop from deeply colored foods like tomato sauce, curry, or red wine reductions. These marks don't affect performance or flavor — in fact, many seasoned cooks see them as a badge of experience. But if you prefer to keep your enamel bright, an occasional deep clean with baking soda or the manufacturer's cleaner will keep it looking nearly new.

What Not to Do When Cleaning

Caring for your Le Creuset means knowing not just what to do, but what *not* to do. The enamel is tough but not indestructible, and a few simple mistakes can cause permanent damage over time. Let's go over the most common pitfalls — and how to avoid them.

The first and most important rule: **never shock your Dutch oven with sudden temperature changes.** Pouring cold water into a hot pot can cause thermal stress, which might crack or craze the enamel. Always allow your cookware to cool before cleaning.

Second, **avoid abrasive tools or cleaners.** Steel wool, metal brushes, or harsh scouring powders can scratch and dull the enamel surface. Once the surface is scratched, it becomes harder to clean and more prone to discoloration. Stick to non-abrasive sponges, silicone tools, and mild cleaners.

Third, **don't use bleach or chlorine-based products.** While these might seem tempting for removing stains, they can erode the enamel and leave behind a chalky residue that discolors the surface. Instead, use natural methods like baking soda or white vinegar for deep cleaning.

Fourth, **never put your Le Creuset in the dishwasher regularly.** While technically dishwasher safe, frequent dishwasher use can dull the enamel's shine and wear down the finish over time. The high heat and strong detergents are too harsh for regular care. Occasional dishwasher cleaning is fine in a pinch, but handwashing is always the gentler and safer choice.

Fifth, **avoid stacking or banging your Dutch oven with other heavy cookware.** The enamel, while strong, can chip if it hits another hard surface. When storing, place a soft cloth or paper towel between the lid and the pot, and if stacking with other pieces, cushion them to prevent scratching.

Another common mistake is leaving water or food residue sitting in the pot for long periods. This can lead to mineral deposits, discoloration, or unpleasant odors. Always clean and dry thoroughly before storing.

And finally, **don't use your Dutch oven as a storage container** for acidic or salty foods. The enamel is non-reactive, but prolonged contact with acidic ingredients like tomato sauce or brine can cause dulling or subtle flavor changes. Once your dish is cooled, transfer leftovers to glass or stainless steel containers.

By avoiding these missteps, you're not just protecting your investment — you're ensuring that your Dutch oven stays functional, beautiful, and ready for another generation of cooking memories.

Reviving Dull Enamel

Over time, even the most lovingly cared-for Le Creuset Dutch oven can lose a bit of its original shine. Maybe the once-glossy interior looks slightly matte, or the exterior colors have dulled after years of use. This doesn't mean your pot is worn out — it just needs a little rejuvenation. Reviving the enamel is easier than you might think, and with a few simple steps, you can bring back that luminous glow that makes Le Creuset pieces so special.

The first step is a gentle polish. Start by cleaning your pot thoroughly with warm, soapy water and a soft sponge. Rinse and dry completely. Once it's clean, use Le

Creuset's enamel cleaner or a homemade mix of baking soda and water (one part soda to one part water). Apply it with a soft cloth and rub gently in circular motions across the enamel surface. This removes surface film, light stains, and mineral deposits while restoring gloss.

If the inside of your pot has developed a light haze — common after repeated use at high temperatures — a soak in a vinegar solution can help. Mix equal parts water and white vinegar, fill the pot halfway, and bring it to a gentle simmer for about 10 minutes. Let it cool, then rinse thoroughly. The mild acid in the vinegar helps dissolve mineral buildup and leaves the enamel refreshed.

To protect that renewed finish, dry the pot completely and, if you wish, lightly coat the rim (where the lid rests) with a tiny dab of vegetable oil to prevent moisture from dulling the edge or causing rust spots on the bare iron rim.

One of the best habits for maintaining shine long-term is consistent gentle cleaning. Every few weeks, give your pot a polish with baking soda paste or the manufacturer's cleaner, even if it doesn't look dirty. This preventive care keeps residue from building up and maintains the enamel's mirror-like surface.

If your pot has developed minor dull patches on the interior from years of cooking acidic foods, don't worry — this doesn't affect its performance. The enamel remains safe and non-reactive. Over time, these faint marks simply become part of your Dutch oven's character, a visual record of the countless meals it's helped you create.

What's truly remarkable about Le Creuset's enamel is how well it endures. With minimal effort, you can keep it looking elegant and vibrant for decades — a piece that not only functions perfectly but also retains its beauty and charm as it ages.

CHAPTER 8

PROTECTING AND STORING

There's a certain beauty in lifting the lid off your Le Creuset Dutch oven after years of use and seeing that it still gleams — a familiar, well-loved piece that looks as good as it cooks. While the pot itself is famously durable, how you handle and store it between meals plays a big part in how long it keeps that flawless finish. Protecting your Dutch oven isn't about fussiness or over-caution — it's about developing small, mindful habits that ensure your cookware remains both functional and beautiful for decades.

Think of your Le Creuset as more than just a cooking tool; it's a lifelong companion in your culinary journey. It's been fired at over 1,400°F during manufacturing, designed to withstand oven heat, stovetop flame, and countless stews, breads, and roasts. But like any high-quality item, even the toughest enamel surface benefits from thoughtful care. It can chip if dropped, scratch if mishandled, or lose a bit of shine if stored improperly. Fortunately, all of these issues are easily preventable once you know how.

This chapter will walk you through exactly how to protect your Dutch oven's enamel, store it safely, and handle its parts — the lid, knobs, and accessories — with care. Whether your pot sits proudly on the stovetop as a centerpiece or rests in a cupboard between Sunday dinners, these methods will help it stay in pristine condition, ready for your next inspired meal.

How to Prevent Chipping and Scratches

Let's begin with the most common concern for any enameled cast iron owner: chips and scratches. The enamel coating on your Le Creuset is one of the brand's signature features — tough, glass-smooth, and non-reactive — but it's still glass at its core. That means, like glass, it can chip if it experiences sharp impact or abrasive friction. The good news? These chips and scratches are almost always preventable with mindful handling and a few easy habits.

The first and most important rule is **handle with care when moving your Dutch oven.** Never drag it across a hard surface, like a granite countertop or stovetop grate. Always lift it with both hands, supporting the base with one and gripping the handle with the other. Even a small scrape across a rough surface can dull the enamel over time.

When cooking, be gentle with your utensils. Stick to silicone, wooden, or heat-resistant plastic spoons and spatulas. Metal utensils — particularly sharp-edged ones like forks, whisks, or tongs — can leave faint surface marks on the enamel interior. These aren't usually deep scratches, but repeated use can dull the surface or create visible scuffing. Think of your pot as a smooth canvas — you want to preserve that seamless coating for both appearance and longevity.

Next, avoid stacking heavy pots or pans inside your Le Creuset. While it might seem convenient to save space, the weight of other cookware can cause micro-abrasions or even small chips if the metal edges rub against the enamel. If you need to stack (for instance, multiple Le Creuset pieces), always use a protective barrier — a soft cloth, paper towel, or pan protector — between them.

Be cautious of thermal shock, too. Just as with cleaning, rapid temperature changes can stress the enamel. Pouring cold liquid into a hot Dutch oven or transferring it straight from oven to fridge can lead to cracking or fine fissures in the enamel. Always let your pot cool gradually before rinsing or refrigerating, and bring refrigerated dishes closer to room temperature before reheating them in the oven.

If you ever do notice a small chip on the rim or lid edge, don't panic. Chips on the unglazed edges — such as the top rim where the lid rests — are usually cosmetic and don't affect cooking performance. Just make sure to dry those areas thoroughly after washing to prevent rust on the exposed cast iron underneath. For chips on the interior enamel, which are rare with careful use, avoid cooking acidic or salty foods in that spot, as it could cause discoloration or mild corrosion over time.

Lastly, a good preventive habit is to **rotate your Dutch oven when storing or cooking** — meaning, don't always bang the same handle or rim against a shelf, hook, or lid. Tiny dings add up over years. Treat it with the same consideration you would a fine piece of stoneware or glass — durable, but deserving of respect.

When you make these small adjustments to how you use and move your pot, you'll find that chips and scratches become almost nonexistent. The payoff? Your Le Creuset will retain its signature glossy finish — that beautiful, luminous surface that first drew you to it — for generations.

Proper Storage Methods

After cooking and cleaning, proper storage is your Dutch oven's quiet guardian. It might not seem as critical as temperature control or cleaning methods, but the way you store your pot directly affects its enamel, moisture balance, and even how convenient it is to use the next time. Think of storage as the final step in the cooking cycle — a brief pause before your next masterpiece begins.

Start with one simple rule: **your Dutch oven should always be clean and completely dry before storing.** Even tiny traces of moisture can leave mineral spots or, worse, cause light rusting on the unglazed rim or lid edges where the cast iron is exposed. After washing, towel dry thoroughly, then leave it uncovered on the counter for an hour or two to air out before putting it away.

When it comes to *where* to store it, choose a cool, dry area away from moisture and direct sunlight. Excess humidity (like that from a dishwasher vent or a damp cupboard near a sink) can affect the finish over time. Direct sunlight can fade the outer enamel color, especially the lighter shades. A dedicated shelf, cabinet, or sturdy kitchen island drawer is ideal.

Many owners like to display their Le Creuset proudly on an open rack or stove. If you do, make sure it's not placed near a heat source where grease or steam might settle on the surface — that can create a sticky film over time. A quick wipe every week keeps it fresh and ready to use.

When storing with the lid on, there's an important detail many overlook: **don't seal it tightly.** Trapped moisture can lead to odor buildup or a faint mustiness, especially if your kitchen is humid. Instead, place the lid slightly ajar or wedge a paper towel between the pot and lid to allow airflow. This small habit keeps the interior smelling clean and fresh.

If you own several pieces of enameled cookware, you might be tempted to nest them to save space. This is fine if done correctly, but always cushion between layers. Use pan protectors, soft cloth napkins, or felt pads to prevent friction between enamel surfaces. Never let metal handles or rims press directly against another piece — that's how chips happen.

You can also hang your Dutch oven by its handles if you have a strong enough wall-mounted rack or pot rail, though be sure the support can handle the weight. The key is stability — if there's even a small chance the pot could bump or swing into another piece, it's better to store it on a flat shelf.

For those who like to leave their Le Creuset on the stovetop for easy access (a common practice in many kitchens), make sure it's placed on a clean, cool burner. Rotate it occasionally so one handle isn't always exposed to heat or sunlight, and keep the lid slightly off to prevent condensation.

The bottom line: treat storage as an act of preservation, not just organization. When your Dutch oven is stored properly — clean, dry, cushioned, and ventilated — it rewards you every time you take it out, looking as vibrant and ready as the day you bought it.

Handling Lids, Knobs, and Accessories Safely

Your Le Creuset Dutch oven isn't just about the pot itself — it's a thoughtfully designed system of parts that work together seamlessly. The lid traps moisture and flavor, the knob gives you control, and accessories like silicone handles or trivets make cooking and serving more comfortable. Each of these deserves a bit of care to stay in top condition.

Let's start with the lid. It's beautifully heavy and perfectly fitted, but that weight means it can easily chip the rim of your pot if set down carelessly. Always lift and place the lid gently — never drop it or twist it forcefully into position. When removing a hot lid, tilt it slightly away from you to let steam escape safely before setting it down on a trivet or heat-safe surface. Avoid placing it directly on a cold countertop, which can cause temperature shock and risk cracking the enamel underside.

When storing, resist the urge to rest the lid upside down inside the pot, especially if the edges touch enamel-to-enamel. That small pressure point can cause scratching or dull spots. Instead, either store the lid upright beside the pot or use a soft cloth or paper towel as a buffer between them.

Now, about the **knobs**. Le Creuset knobs are designed to withstand oven heat — most stainless-steel knobs are safe up to 500°F, while the standard phenolic knobs (the black plastic-like ones) can handle up to around 375°F. Always check your model's specifications before placing the lid in the oven. If you often cook at higher temperatures, you might consider upgrading to the metal knob for maximum versatility.

To clean knobs, simply handwash them with warm, soapy water. If grease or residue builds up around the screw area, gently remove the knob using a screwdriver (while the lid is cool) and clean both parts separately before reassembling. Don't overtighten when reattaching — snug is sufficient.

Accessories like silicone handle covers, trivets, and spoon rests also benefit from routine care. Wash them in warm, soapy water and dry completely. If you use silicone handle sleeves during cooking, remember that they can get hot over time, so always check before gripping. Store them in a drawer near your Dutch oven so they're always handy when needed.

Another important consideration is **how you transport your Dutch oven** — whether moving it from oven to table or from one kitchen to another. Always use both hands and ensure you have a stable, heat-safe surface ready before setting it down. Never balance the lid loosely on top while carrying; the weight and movement could cause it to slip off.

If you ever use accessories like metal trivets or racks inside your pot (for baking or roasting), make sure they're enamel-safe and free from rough edges that could scratch the interior. Le Creuset makes compatible inserts that protect the enamel while offering versatility.

By treating each part — lid, knob, and accessory — with care and intention, you extend the life of the entire set. These small details might seem minor, but they make all the difference in preserving the perfect fit and flawless look that Le Creuset is known for.

CHAPTER 9

TROUBLESHOOTING COMMON PROBLEMS

No matter how careful or seasoned you are in the kitchen, even the most experienced cooks occasionally face a stubborn bit of stuck food, an unexpected discoloration, or a moment of worry when their prized cookware doesn't look quite as pristine as it once did. The truth is, owning a Le Creuset Dutch oven isn't about perfection — it's about *practice*, and with practice comes the occasional hiccup. These moments aren't setbacks; they're opportunities to learn how this remarkable piece of cookware behaves and how to keep it performing flawlessly for decades.

The beauty of Le Creuset lies in its resilience. Unlike cheaper, nonstick pots that lose their coating after a few uses or cast iron pans that require endless seasoning, your enameled Dutch oven is engineered to bounce back. The key is simply understanding what's happening when something doesn't go as planned. If food sticks, it's not because you've "ruined" the enamel — it's usually a matter of heat management or technique. If the interior looks discolored after a rich stew or curry, it's not permanent damage — it's the natural patina that develops from cooking flavorful food. And when you're truly unsure, Le Creuset's customer support is there to back you up with professional care and warranty coverage.

This chapter will help you become fluent in your Dutch oven's quirks — what causes them, how to fix them, and how to prevent them from recurring. By the end, you'll not only solve the common issues most owners face but also gain a deeper confidence in your ability to handle your Le Creuset like a pro.

Why Food Sticks (and How to Fix It)

Few things frustrate a cook more than lifting the lid to find that the beautiful golden crust of your chicken has instead glued itself stubbornly to the bottom of your Dutch oven. When food sticks, it can feel like something went wrong — but in truth, it's often just the result of timing or temperature. Le Creuset's enamel surface isn't nonstick in the traditional, Teflon-coated sense; rather, it relies on proper preheating, oiling, and temperature control to achieve that ideal release.

The most common reason food sticks is cooking at too low or too high a temperature. If the pot isn't hot enough before you add your ingredients, proteins will bond with the enamel surface instead of searing cleanly. Conversely, if the pot is *too* hot, the surface oil can burn before the food even has a chance to release, causing scorching or carbonized residue that clings to the enamel. The sweet spot is medium to medium-high heat — hot enough to sear, but not so hot that oil begins to smoke.

Here's a simple trick to test for readiness: before adding oil, heat your Dutch oven for two to three minutes on medium heat, then add a few drops of water. If they dance and evaporate instantly, the pot is ready. Add your oil, swirl it evenly, and let it heat for another 15–30 seconds before introducing food. Proper preheating creates a microscopic cushion of vapor between the food and the enamel, allowing for that signature golden-brown crust and easy release.

Another culprit is using too little oil or fat. While Le Creuset's enamel allows you to cook with less oil than traditional cast iron, it still needs a thin layer to prevent sticking — especially for proteins like chicken, eggs, or fish. Think of oil not as an afterthought but as a functional layer that helps conduct heat evenly and protect the enamel.

If you've already found yourself with a stuck-on mess, don't panic. Most of the time, it's easy to fix without scrubbing or harsh cleaners. Start by deglazing — pour in a bit of warm water, broth, or wine while the pot is still warm (not hot), and gently scrape with a wooden spatula. The liquid will loosen the caramelized bits — known as fond — which, conveniently, also happens to be packed with flavor. Use it to build a sauce, and you've turned a problem into perfection.

For tougher residues, fill the pot with warm water and a spoonful of baking soda. Let it soak for 15–20 minutes, then use a soft sponge or nylon scrubber to gently remove the remaining food. Avoid steel wool or abrasive pads — they can dull the enamel's surface over time.

It's also worth noting that different foods behave differently in enamel. Acidic dishes like tomato sauce or citrus-based marinades rarely stick because the moisture and acidity help break down proteins. Dry-seared meats, on the other hand, need a bit more attention and fat. Once you understand how each food type interacts with the enamel, sticking becomes less of a mystery and more of a manageable quirk.

Over time, as your pot develops a slight cooking patina — a thin, invisible film that naturally builds up from use — you'll find that food releases more easily. This isn't damage; it's character. In fact, many long-time Le Creuset owners consider it a sign of a well-loved and well-seasoned pot, even though it's technically enamel, not bare cast iron.

In short, sticking isn't failure — it's feedback. Your Dutch oven is teaching you how to master heat, timing, and technique. With patience and practice, you'll find that those once-sticky meals become perfectly seared masterpieces every time.

Discoloration and Stain Removal Tips

After a few hearty stews, braised meats, or tomato-based sauces, you might notice that your once-bright enamel interior has dulled a bit or taken on a slight tint. This is perfectly normal. The pale interior enamel of Le Creuset is designed to show cooking progress — it's part of what makes it so practical — but it also means it's more prone to visible stains. These discolorations are harmless, but if you prefer that fresh, cream-colored look, there are easy ways to restore it.

Let's start with prevention. The best way to minimize staining is to clean promptly after cooking. Allow your Dutch oven to cool to a warm (not hot) temperature, fill it with warm water and a drop of dish soap, and let it soak for 10–15 minutes. This loosens any food residue and keeps pigments from setting in. Avoid letting food sit overnight, especially highly pigmented ingredients like turmeric, tomato paste, red wine, or soy sauce.

But what if the stains have already settled in? Don't worry — the solution is both simple and gentle. One of the most effective methods is a baking soda paste. Mix two tablespoons of baking soda with a little warm water to form a thick paste. Spread it over the stained area, let it sit for 10–20 minutes, then scrub gently with a non-abrasive sponge. Rinse thoroughly and dry. You'll be amazed at how much brightness this simple method can restore.

For more stubborn discoloration — like those golden-brown rings from simmered sauces — you can try a baking soda soak. Fill the pot halfway with warm water, add two tablespoons of baking soda, and bring it to a gentle simmer on the stove for 10–15 minutes. Turn off the heat and let the water cool completely before washing. This loosens even the toughest cooked-on stains without harming the enamel.

Another safe and highly effective cleaner is Le Creuset's own cast iron cleaner, formulated specifically for enamel care. It works particularly well for maintaining the pot's glossy sheen without harsh abrasives. A pea-sized amount on a damp sponge is usually all you need.

Avoid using bleach or highly acidic cleaners — they can dull the enamel finish over time and weaken its smooth texture. Similarly, steer clear of metal scrubbers or scouring powders. While they might seem tempting for fast results, they actually leave micro-scratches that can make future staining worse.

If you notice a brownish tint on the bottom that doesn't fade even after thorough cleaning, that's likely a heat tint — a natural byproduct of caramelization and Maillard browning during cooking. It's not a flaw; in fact, it's common among experienced Le Creuset users and doesn't affect performance or flavor. Some cooks even appreciate the faint patina as a badge of culinary experience — proof that their Dutch oven has seen many delicious meals.

For external stains — like oil splatters or residue on the outer enamel — a damp cloth with dish soap usually does the trick. For tougher spots, try a gentle rub with a Magic Eraser or a paste of baking soda and water. Always rinse and dry thoroughly to preserve that iconic shine.

The secret to a spotless Le Creuset isn't perfectionism; it's consistency. A little routine care after each use keeps stains at bay, and the occasional deep clean restores your Dutch oven's glow. Remember, a few marks or tints are not signs of wear — they're the culinary equivalent of laugh lines: evidence of good times, good food, and countless memories made around the table.

When to Contact Le Creuset Support

While Le Creuset cookware is famously durable, there are rare occasions when you might encounter an issue that cleaning or care alone can't fix. That's when the brand's outstanding customer support comes in — one of the reasons Le Creuset has built such a loyal following for nearly a century.

The first thing to know is that Le Creuset offers a limited lifetime warranty on its enameled cast iron cookware. This warranty covers defects in materials and workmanship — meaning, if something goes wrong due to a flaw in manufacturing, Le Creuset will repair or replace your piece free of charge. It doesn't cover damage from misuse or normal wear and tear, but the company's definition of "defect" is fairly generous, especially when you can provide clear photos or proof of purchase.

So, how do you know when it's time to contact them? Here are the most common situations:

- **Cracking or crazing in the enamel** that wasn't caused by dropping or sudden temperature shock.

- **Chips or flakes on the interior cooking surface** that appear without impact.

- **Uneven enamel application or bubbling** that becomes visible after a few uses.

- **Lid or knob defects**, such as separation, warping, or thread damage.

- **Rust formation on the rim** that doesn't resolve with proper cleaning and drying.

Before reaching out, it's worth taking a few photos of the issue in good lighting, showing the whole pot and the affected area clearly. Le Creuset's website has an online claims portal where you can submit these images along with your product details and purchase information. In many cases, they'll offer to replace the pot or provide a store credit toward a new one.

It's also reassuring to know that Le Creuset's support team is genuinely responsive and knowledgeable. They understand that their cookware isn't just a product — it's an investment and often an emotional one. Many owners have shared stories of receiving replacement pieces for items they've owned for years, simply because the company stands behind its craftsmanship.

If your issue isn't covered under warranty — say, you accidentally chipped the enamel by dropping the lid — don't despair. Le Creuset can still provide advice on safe continued use or direct you to professional repair services if applicable. In some cases, minor exterior chips can be safely smoothed and sealed, allowing you to keep cooking without risk.

Reaching out for support doesn't mean you've failed in caring for your cookware; it means you value it enough to seek expert help. And that's exactly what Le Creuset's customer service is there for — to ensure your Dutch oven continues to bring you joy, confidence, and beautiful meals for a lifetime.

CHAPTER 10

EASY EVERYDAY RECIPES

If there's one thing that truly brings a Le Creuset Dutch oven to life, it's the moment you cook your first full meal in it. That first simmering stew or loaf of bread isn't just food — it's an experience. The sound of a slow bubble, the comforting weight of the lid, the way the aromas build and mingle until your kitchen smells like something out of a cozy countryside inn — that's when it clicks. You realize this isn't just a pot. It's a vessel of transformation.

What makes the Dutch oven so magical is its versatility. With one piece of cookware, you can sear, sauté, braise, bake, and simmer. You can take it from stovetop to oven without switching pans. And best of all, it doesn't just cook your food — it *develops* it. The tight-fitting lid traps moisture and flavor, creating dishes that taste richer and more complex than they ever would in a regular pot. Meals that once required hours of babysitting can now be made effortlessly, with the Dutch oven quietly doing most of the work while you go about your day.

This chapter is designed to be your starting point — a small but powerful collection of simple, timeless recipes that highlight exactly what your Le Creuset does best. These are the kind of meals you'll come back to again and again: cozy stews, creamy one-pot dinners, hearty chilis, and that rustic loaf of bread that makes you feel like a true artisan baker. Each recipe is straightforward enough for beginners, yet produces results that feel restaurant-worthy.

By the time you finish this chapter, your Dutch oven won't feel like a new kitchen gadget anymore — it'll feel like an old friend.

Classic Beef Stew

There's something profoundly comforting about a pot of beef stew bubbling gently on the stove. It's the kind of meal that warms your hands as much as your heart — tender chunks of beef, silky vegetables, and a savory gravy that tastes like it's been simmering for hours, even if it hasn't. Your Le Creuset Dutch oven is tailor-made for this kind of dish because it distributes heat evenly and maintains a steady simmer, ensuring every bite is melt-in-your-mouth perfect.

Start with about two pounds of beef chuck, cut into large cubes. Pat them dry with paper towels — this step matters more than most realize. Moisture is the enemy of a good sear, and that deep caramelized crust on the beef is what gives the stew its rich, layered flavor. Heat your Dutch oven over medium-high and add a tablespoon of oil. When it shimmers, sear the beef in batches. Don't crowd the pot — give each piece room to brown beautifully. The fond, those browned bits left behind, will be the base of your flavor.

Once the beef is seared and set aside, reduce the heat slightly and toss in chopped onions, carrots, and celery. Sauté them for about five minutes until they soften and pick up that golden color from the fond. Add a tablespoon of tomato paste and cook it for a minute or two — this deepens the flavor and gives your stew that gorgeous mahogany hue.

Deglaze the pot with a generous splash of red wine (or beef broth if you prefer). Scrape up every last bit of the browned goodness from the bottom. Then, add the beef back in along with three cups of broth, a couple of bay leaves, thyme, and a small spoonful of Worcestershire sauce. Bring it to a simmer, cover with the lid, and reduce the heat to low. The heavy cast iron and tight-fitting lid will work together to create an even, moist environment where the beef tenderizes naturally.

After about 90 minutes, the meat should be fork-tender and the broth luxuriously thickened. Taste and adjust the seasoning — a little salt and pepper can make all the difference here. Serve it with crusty bread or over mashed potatoes, and you'll understand why the Dutch oven is the ultimate tool for comfort food.

Creamy Chicken and Vegetables

If beef stew is comfort in a bowl, creamy chicken and vegetables are comfort with a touch of elegance. This dish feels like something you'd order at a country bistro — hearty yet refined, creamy yet not heavy. The Le Creuset Dutch oven excels here because it allows you to build flavor step by step, without ever needing to switch pans.

Start by heating your pot over medium heat with a drizzle of olive oil and a tablespoon of butter. Season four bone-in chicken thighs (or breasts, if you prefer) with salt and pepper, and place them skin-side down to sear. You'll hear that satisfying sizzle as the skin crisps up. After about six minutes per side, the chicken should be golden and aromatic. Remove and set aside.

Next, in the same pot, sauté diced onions, garlic, and sliced carrots until they soften and begin to caramelize. You can add mushrooms here if you like — they soak up the flavors beautifully. Sprinkle in a spoonful of flour and stir to create a roux. Then pour in two cups of chicken broth, stirring constantly to thicken the sauce.

Add a cup of cream (or half-and-half for a lighter version) and a sprig of fresh thyme. Nestle the chicken back into the pot, making sure the sauce covers it about halfway. Cover and let it simmer gently for 25–30 minutes on low heat. The enamel surface of your Dutch oven ensures nothing burns or sticks, even during a slow simmer.

When the chicken is fully cooked and the sauce has reduced slightly, stir in a handful of peas or spinach for color and freshness. The result is a velvety, savory dish that tastes like a cozy Sunday dinner but takes less than an hour to make.

Serve it over rice, pasta, or simply with crusty bread to mop up the sauce. The beauty of this recipe is that it adapts to your fridge — substitute whatever vegetables you have on hand, and it'll still taste amazing. That's the charm of Dutch oven cooking: it's forgiving, flavorful, and always deeply satisfying.

Simple Homemade Chili

A good pot of chili is the very definition of comfort food — warm, filling, and endlessly customizable. The Dutch oven shines here because its heat retention creates the perfect slow-cooking environment where flavors meld naturally and beans turn tender without falling apart.

Begin by heating your Dutch oven over medium-high and adding a bit of oil. Toss in one pound of ground beef (or turkey, or even plant-based crumbles for a vegetarian twist). Brown it thoroughly, breaking it apart as it cooks. Once it's fully browned, remove it and set aside, then sauté diced onions, bell peppers, and garlic until soft.

Add two tablespoons of tomato paste and your spices: chili powder, cumin, paprika, and a pinch of cayenne for heat. Let them bloom in the oil for 30 seconds — this releases their aroma and depth. Then, add the cooked meat back in, followed by one can of diced tomatoes, one can of tomato sauce, a cup of broth, and a can of kidney or black beans (rinsed and drained). Stir well, bring it to a boil, and then reduce the heat to low.

Cover and let it simmer for at least 45 minutes, stirring occasionally. The even heat of the Dutch oven ensures nothing sticks or scorches on the bottom, even with thick sauces. As it cooks, the flavors deepen — the beans absorb the spices, and the sauce takes on a silky consistency.

When it's done, taste and adjust the seasoning. A splash of lime juice or a sprinkle of sugar can balance acidity. You can also stir in a bit of dark chocolate or espresso powder if you want a richer, smoky flavor — both secret tricks of seasoned chili lovers.

Serve your chili hot, with your favorite toppings: shredded cheese, sour cream, chopped green onions, or even a handful of tortilla chips for crunch. What's remarkable about chili is how well it reheats — the next day, it somehow tastes even better. Your Le Creuset makes enough to feed a crowd, and cleanup is simple since the enamel wipes clean effortlessly.

This chili is your go-to for game nights, cozy weekends, or quick weeknight dinners that feel like they took all day.

No-Knead Artisan Bread

Now for one of the most magical things your Dutch oven can do: bake bread. Yes, the same pot you used for stews and soups can turn out a bakery-quality loaf with a crisp golden crust and a soft, chewy interior. No kneading, no complicated steps — just time, patience, and a bit of trust in the process.

The secret to this bread lies in steam. When baked in a Dutch oven, the lid traps steam from the dough, mimicking the effect of professional steam ovens used in bakeries. That's what creates that signature crackly crust.

Start by whisking together three cups of all-purpose flour, one teaspoon of salt, and a half teaspoon of instant yeast in a large bowl. Add one and a half cups of warm water and stir with a spoon until it forms a sticky dough. Cover the bowl with plastic wrap or a damp towel and let it rest at room temperature for 12 to 18 hours. This long fermentation develops flavor and gluten naturally — no kneading needed.

When you're ready to bake, preheat your oven to 450°F (230°C) with your Dutch oven inside (lid on) for at least 30 minutes. Meanwhile, turn the dough out onto a floured surface, shape it loosely into a ball, and let it rest on parchment paper while the pot heats.

Carefully remove the Dutch oven — it'll be scorching hot — and lift the dough (with the parchment) right into it. Cover and bake for 30 minutes. Then remove the lid and bake for another 10–15 minutes until the crust turns a deep golden brown.

When you lift the lid, you'll see something extraordinary: a loaf that looks and tastes like it came from an artisan bakery. The crust will crackle as it cools, and the inside will be perfectly airy. Let it rest at least 30 minutes before slicing — this helps the interior set and prevents it from becoming gummy.

This bread pairs beautifully with all the recipes you've made so far — from beef stew to chili. It's also wonderful on its own, smeared with butter or dipped in olive oil. And once you've made it once, you'll find yourself doing it again and again, experimenting with herbs, cheese, or whole grains.

There's something deeply satisfying about making bread in a Dutch oven. It's the purest example of what this cookware represents — simplicity, patience, and incredible results.

CHAPTER 11

WEEKEND & SPECIAL OCCASION DISHES

There's something magical about weekends — a slower rhythm, softer light, and a little more room to savor life. The weekdays are for quick meals, efficient cooking, and getting everyone fed. But weekends? Those are for lingering in the kitchen, for letting aromas fill the air, and for cooking dishes that mean something. Whether it's celebrating a milestone, hosting friends, or simply indulging in a quiet, cozy evening, your Le Creuset Dutch oven was made for these kinds of meals.

This chapter is your invitation to slow down and cook with intention. It's about dishes that fill the house with deep, layered scents — the kind that make your family wander into the kitchen asking, "What's cooking?" These are recipes that turn the act of cooking into a small celebration. They might take a little longer, but they reward you in every way: tender meat that falls apart at the touch of a fork, sauces that taste like they simmered all day, and textures that feel as luxurious as they taste.

Le Creuset Dutch ovens were designed for precisely this kind of cooking — where time and care create something extraordinary. Their even heat distribution ensures perfect braises; their tight-fitting lids lock in moisture, transforming inexpensive cuts into melt-in-your-mouth masterpieces. And their elegant, oven-to-table design makes them ideal for presentation. You can cook, serve, and impress — all in the same stunning piece of cookware.

In this chapter, we'll explore four dishes that have become synonymous with comfort and celebration alike. From the classic French *Coq au Vin* and deeply flavorful braised short ribs to the nostalgic creaminess of baked mac and cheese and the hearty indulgence of Dutch oven lasagna, these recipes will show you just how far your Dutch oven can take you. So pour yourself a glass of wine, put on some music, and let's turn your kitchen into a sanctuary of flavor.

Coq au Vin (French Wine-Braised Chicken)

Few dishes embody rustic French cooking as beautifully as *Coq au Vin*. It's humble yet sophisticated, a dish that transforms simple ingredients — chicken, wine, onions, and mushrooms — into something transcendent. It's a perfect example of what your Dutch oven was made for: slow, gentle cooking that coaxes every ounce of flavor from the ingredients.

Begin with a whole chicken cut into pieces, or simply use bone-in thighs and drumsticks. Pat them dry and season with salt and pepper. In your Le Creuset Dutch oven, cook several strips of chopped bacon over medium heat until crisp. Remove the bacon with a slotted spoon, leaving the flavorful fat behind.

Next, add your chicken pieces to the pot in batches, browning them on all sides until golden. Don't rush this part — it's where the foundation of flavor begins. Once browned, transfer the chicken to a plate and add chopped onions, carrots, and garlic to the pot. Sauté until softened and aromatic, then sprinkle in a tablespoon of flour to thicken the eventual sauce.

Now for the star ingredient: red wine. Traditionally, Burgundy is used, but any good dry red wine will do. Pour in about two cups and stir, scraping up the flavorful bits from the bottom of the pot. Add the chicken back along with thyme, bay leaves, and a cup of chicken broth. Bring it to a gentle simmer, then cover and let it braise on low heat for 45 minutes to an hour.

As it cooks, your kitchen will fill with the kind of aroma that stops conversations — a deep, savory perfume of wine, herbs, and roasted chicken. In the final 15 minutes, stir in sautéed mushrooms and pearl onions for a classic touch. When it's ready, the chicken should be tender enough to pull apart with a fork, and the sauce should be glossy and rich.

Serve your *Coq au Vin* with mashed potatoes, buttered noodles, or a chunk of crusty bread to soak up every drop of that luxurious sauce. It's not a complicated dish — it just asks for a little patience. And with your Dutch oven, patience always pays off.

Braised Short Ribs with Red Wine

If *Coq au Vin* is elegance in a pot, then braised short ribs are pure indulgence. This dish is the definition of comfort — hearty, rich, and so tender that the meat falls away from the bone with the slightest touch. It's the kind of meal you make when you want to impress someone or treat yourself after a long week.

Start with four to six bone-in short ribs, each generously seasoned with salt and pepper. Heat your Le Creuset over medium-high and add a splash of oil. When the oil shimmers, sear the ribs in batches until each side develops a deep, brown crust. This caramelization is key to flavor, so resist the temptation to move them too soon. Once all sides are beautifully seared, remove the ribs and set them aside.

Next, add diced onions, carrots, and celery — the classic *mirepoix* — to the pot. Sauté for several minutes until the vegetables soften and pick up the flavorful browned bits from the bottom. Add a few cloves of minced garlic and cook briefly before stirring in a tablespoon of tomato paste. Let it darken slightly to deepen its flavor.

Pour in two cups of robust red wine, preferably something full-bodied like Cabernet Sauvignon or Syrah. Stir well, scraping up the fond from the bottom. Then add about two cups of beef broth, a couple of sprigs of rosemary, and two bay leaves. Return the ribs to the pot, nestling them into the liquid. They should be mostly submerged — if not, add a bit more broth.

Bring the liquid to a simmer, cover with the lid, and transfer the Dutch oven to a preheated 325°F (160°C) oven. Let it cook undisturbed for about 2½ to 3 hours. During this time, something magical happens: the collagen in the meat breaks down, transforming the ribs into fork-tender perfection. The sauce thickens and develops that deep, luxurious sheen that only comes from slow braising.

Once done, remove the ribs carefully — they'll be so tender they might fall apart. Skim any excess fat from the surface and taste the sauce. You can strain it for a smoother texture or leave it rustic. Either way, it's pure decadence.

Serve the ribs over creamy mashed potatoes, polenta, or even buttered egg noodles. A sprinkle of fresh parsley adds color and brightness. The beauty of this dish is that it tastes even better the next day — the flavors meld overnight, making it ideal for entertaining ahead of time.

Baked Mac & Cheese

Sometimes, the best special occasion dish isn't fancy at all — it's just pure, comforting bliss. Few foods evoke nostalgia like baked mac and cheese, and when made in your Le Creuset, it becomes something truly extraordinary. The heavy, enameled cast iron creates even heat for a perfectly golden crust, while its deep sides allow for plenty of that creamy, cheesy goodness inside.

Begin by cooking a pound of pasta — elbow macaroni or cavatappi work beautifully — just until al dente. Drain and set aside. In your Dutch oven, melt four tablespoons of butter over medium heat, then whisk in an equal amount of flour to make a roux. Stir constantly for about a minute until the mixture turns lightly golden and smells nutty.

Gradually whisk in four cups of warm milk, a little at a time, until the mixture is smooth and thickened. This is your béchamel base — creamy, luscious, and the perfect canvas for cheese. Lower the heat and stir in two cups of shredded sharp cheddar, one cup of Gruyère, and a handful of Parmesan for depth. Season with salt, pepper, and a pinch of mustard powder or paprika to enhance the flavor.

Add the cooked pasta and stir to coat every piece with that velvety sauce. If you like a bit of crunch, top it with a mixture of breadcrumbs, melted butter, and Parmesan. Place the lid slightly ajar and bake in a preheated 375°F (190°C) oven for about 25–30 minutes, or until the top is golden and bubbling around the edges.

When it emerges from the oven, resist the urge to dive right in. Let it rest for a few minutes — this allows the sauce to set slightly, giving you creamy, cohesive scoops instead of a cheesy flood.

Baked mac and cheese in a Le Creuset is the ultimate crowd-pleaser. It's perfect for family dinners, potlucks, or just a night when you want to indulge. It's also endlessly customizable — you can add crispy bacon, caramelized onions, lobster, or roasted vegetables to make it your own. Whatever variation you choose, one thing's for sure: you'll never go back to boxed mac again.

Dutch Oven Lasagna

Lasagna might not be the first dish that comes to mind when you think of a Dutch oven, but once you try it, you'll never make it any other way. The Dutch oven's even heat and tight seal create a perfect balance between tender pasta, bubbling sauce, and gooey melted cheese. Plus, it's all made in one pot — from sauce to bake — making cleanup delightfully simple.

Start by making the sauce directly in your Dutch oven. Heat olive oil over medium heat and sauté chopped onions and garlic until fragrant. Add a pound of ground beef or Italian sausage (or a mix of both) and cook until browned. Stir in a jar of high-quality marinara or your own homemade tomato sauce, a tablespoon of tomato paste, and a splash of red wine for richness. Season with salt, pepper, oregano, and a pinch of sugar to balance the acidity. Let it simmer gently for 15–20 minutes.

Once the sauce is ready, remove half of it from the pot and set it aside. Now it's time to assemble. Layer uncooked lasagna noodles directly over the sauce at the bottom — no need to boil them first; the moisture from the sauce will cook them perfectly. Spread a mixture of ricotta cheese, an egg, and a handful of Parmesan over the noodles. Then add a layer of mozzarella and a ladle of sauce. Repeat until you've used all your ingredients, finishing with sauce and cheese on top.

Cover the pot with its lid and bake at 375°F (190°C) for 45 minutes. Remove the lid and bake for an additional 10–15 minutes until the cheese is golden and bubbling. The Dutch oven's even heat ensures that every layer cooks evenly and the noodles absorb the perfect amount of sauce.

When it's done, let the lasagna rest for at least 15 minutes before slicing — this allows the layers to set and gives you those beautiful, restaurant-quality squares.

Dutch oven lasagna isn't just a clever twist; it's a revelation. The texture is perfectly balanced — soft but not soggy, rich but not heavy. And because it's all cooked and served in one elegant pot, it goes straight from oven to table in style.

CHAPTER 12

HEALTHY & MODERN RECIPES

Cooking with your Le Creuset Dutch oven doesn't always have to mean rich stews or indulgent comfort food. In fact, one of the most rewarding ways to use this versatile pot is to explore dishes that are both nourishing and modern—meals that make you feel as good as they taste. Healthy cooking doesn't mean bland, and it certainly doesn't mean complicated. When you have the right tool, eating well can be as simple, vibrant, and deeply satisfying as any classic recipe.

Over the past few decades, our relationship with food has evolved. We're more aware than ever of what we eat and how it affects our energy, mood, and long-term health. But "healthy" doesn't have to mean giving up comfort or pleasure. In many ways, the Dutch oven is the ideal vessel for this kind of cooking—it locks in nutrients, preserves natural flavors, and minimizes the need for excess fat or oil. Whether you're simmering grains, slow-cooking legumes, or roasting a rainbow of vegetables, your Le Creuset helps you achieve rich flavor and perfect texture with minimal effort.

This chapter celebrates the balance between wholesome and delicious. It's about using fresh, simple ingredients and transforming them into colorful, satisfying meals that fit modern lifestyles. These recipes lean into plant-based goodness, whole grains, and lighter cooking methods while still feeling hearty and fulfilling. Whether you're trying to eat more vegetables, incorporate more plant protein, or simply find flavorful new ways to cook clean, these dishes will show you how easy it can be.

So let's dive in—because when you cook with a Le Creuset, healthy eating doesn't mean restraint; it means abundance: vibrant colors, natural aromas, and the deep, comforting flavors only a Dutch oven can create.

Quinoa Vegetable Stew

If there's one dish that perfectly captures the spirit of modern healthy cooking, it's quinoa vegetable stew. This meal is earthy, comforting, and incredibly versatile—an ideal way to nourish your body while using up whatever vegetables you have on hand. It's a one-pot wonder that feels light but still deeply satisfying, thanks to the nutty heartiness of quinoa and the natural sweetness of slow-simmered vegetables.

To begin, heat a tablespoon of olive oil in your Le Creuset Dutch oven over medium heat. Add chopped onions, carrots, and celery—the classic trio known as mirepoix—and sauté until softened. Add a few cloves of minced garlic and cook just until fragrant. This forms the flavorful foundation of your stew.

Next, stir in a generous handful of chopped vegetables—zucchini, bell peppers, green beans, or even sweet potatoes all work beautifully. Add a cup of rinsed quinoa, which will absorb all the beautiful flavors of the broth as it cooks. Pour in about six cups of vegetable broth, followed by a can of diced tomatoes for richness and acidity. Season with salt, pepper, thyme, and a hint of smoked paprika or cumin for warmth.

Bring the mixture to a gentle boil, then reduce the heat and let it simmer, partially covered, for about 25 minutes. You'll notice the quinoa turning translucent as it cooks and the stew thickening naturally. Stir occasionally to make sure nothing sticks to the bottom.

When the quinoa is tender, stir in a few handfuls of leafy greens like spinach or kale and let them wilt into the stew. A squeeze of fresh lemon juice at the end brightens everything, adding a hint of freshness that balances the hearty base.

What makes this dish so delightful is its flexibility. You can swap ingredients based on the season or your mood. Add lentils for extra protein, top it with avocado slices for creaminess, or sprinkle a little feta or Parmesan on top for a salty finish. The Le Creuset's steady heat ensures every bite is balanced and beautifully textured—comforting yet light, exactly what a modern stew should be.

Mediterranean Chickpea Curry

If you've ever wanted a dish that tastes like sunshine in a bowl, Mediterranean chickpea curry is it. It's colorful, rich in plant protein, and packed with spices that awaken your senses without overwhelming them. This dish is a cross between a stew and a curry—bright, tangy, and deeply satisfying—and it's perfectly suited for your Dutch oven's even, gentle simmering.

Start by warming a couple of tablespoons of olive oil in your Dutch oven over medium heat. Add diced onions and cook until they turn golden and translucent. Stir in minced garlic, followed by spices: ground cumin, coriander, turmeric, paprika, and a pinch of cinnamon. Toasting the spices in oil releases their essential oils, creating that warm, aromatic base that defines Mediterranean-inspired curries.

Next, add two cans of drained chickpeas, stirring them to coat in the fragrant spice mixture. Pour in a can of crushed tomatoes and about a cup of coconut milk for creaminess. If you prefer a lighter dish, you can substitute part of the coconut milk with vegetable broth. Season with salt, pepper, and a splash of lemon juice or red wine vinegar for brightness.

Bring everything to a gentle simmer, then lower the heat and let it bubble slowly for 25 to 30 minutes. As it cooks, the flavors meld beautifully, and the sauce thickens into a luscious, velvety texture. Stir occasionally to prevent sticking, and taste along the way—healthy cooking doesn't have to mean skipping the seasoning.

To finish, fold in a handful of fresh spinach or chopped kale just before serving. The greens will wilt perfectly into the curry, adding extra color and nutrients. A sprinkle of chopped parsley, basil, or even a few crumbles of feta cheese can add an extra layer of freshness and tang.

Serve your chickpea curry over brown rice, farro, or quinoa—or simply enjoy it with warm whole-grain flatbread. The Dutch oven's even heat ensures that every bite tastes deep and complete, with perfectly tender chickpeas and a sauce that feels luxurious yet light. It's a dish that fits right into a healthy modern lifestyle—comforting but not heavy, packed with protein and flavor, and vibrant enough to brighten any day.

Roasted Vegetable Ratatouille

Ratatouille is a dish that celebrates vegetables in all their glory. Originating from the sunny region of Provence, it's a simple yet elegant medley of eggplant, zucchini, bell peppers, onions, and tomatoes—all cooked together until they become tender, fragrant, and irresistibly rich. It's rustic French cooking at its healthiest, and your Le Creuset Dutch oven brings out the best in it.

Start by preheating your oven to 375°F (190°C). Meanwhile, cut your vegetables into even bite-sized chunks—eggplant, zucchini, red and yellow bell peppers, and onions are essential. Heat a drizzle of olive oil in your Dutch oven and sauté the onions and garlic until fragrant. Then add the remaining vegetables, seasoning generously with salt, pepper, thyme, and a splash of balsamic vinegar for a hint of tang.

Stir everything well so the vegetables are coated in oil and herbs, then add a can of diced or crushed tomatoes. Mix again, making sure the sauce is evenly distributed. Cover the pot with the lid and transfer it to the oven. Let it roast for about 45 minutes, stirring once or twice during cooking.

As it bakes, something wonderful happens: the vegetables release their juices, mingle with the tomato base, and slowly caramelize, creating layers of flavor that no quick sauté could ever achieve. The Dutch oven's heat retention ensures that each piece cooks evenly and gently, without losing its shape or color.

Once done, remove the lid and let it roast for an additional 10 to 15 minutes to let some of the liquid evaporate and the edges brown slightly. The result is a stew-like dish that's rich yet light, sweet yet savory—a true celebration of vegetables.

You can enjoy ratatouille warm or at room temperature. It pairs beautifully with whole-grain bread, couscous, or grilled fish, but it's also perfect on its own as a satisfying plant-based main. Drizzle with a little more olive oil and sprinkle with fresh basil or parsley before serving.

Ratatouille is one of those dishes that improves with time, too. Letting it rest overnight allows the flavors to deepen and meld together, making tomorrow's leftovers even better. With your Dutch oven, you'll find that this humble French dish becomes not just a recipe, but a ritual—one that connects you to the pleasure of simple, honest food.

Whole-Grain Dutch Oven Bread

Nothing feels more wholesome—or more rewarding—than baking your own bread. And with your Le Creuset Dutch oven, it's easier and more forgiving than you might imagine. This whole-grain version is hearty, nourishing, and deliciously rustic, perfect for rounding out any meal from this chapter. It's rich in fiber and nutrients but still has that irresistible crisp crust and tender interior that make homemade bread such a joy.

In a large mixing bowl, combine three cups of whole-wheat flour with one cup of all-purpose flour, two teaspoons of salt, and one teaspoon of instant yeast. Stir in about two cups of warm water, mixing until a shaggy dough forms. You don't need to knead this dough vigorously—just stir until everything comes together. Cover the bowl with a towel or plastic wrap and let it rise at room temperature for 10 to 12 hours, or overnight.

When the dough has doubled in size and is dotted with bubbles, gently turn it out onto a floured surface. Fold it over on itself a few times to create surface tension, then shape it into a round loaf. Let it rest for about 30 minutes while you preheat your oven to 450°F (230°C) and place your Dutch oven (with lid) inside to heat up.

When the pot is blazing hot, carefully remove it from the oven and line it with a piece of parchment paper. Gently lower the dough into the pot, cover with the lid, and bake for 30 minutes. Then remove the lid and bake for another 15 minutes, or until the crust is deep golden brown and crisp.

As it cools, the bread will crackle softly—a sound that every baker treasures. When you slice into it, you'll find a tender, flavorful crumb with a nutty aroma from the whole grains. The Dutch oven's sealed environment creates the perfect balance of steam and dry heat, giving you that professional bakery crust without needing special equipment.

This bread is a wholesome base for all your healthy meals. Spread it with avocado, serve it with soups, or simply enjoy it with a drizzle of olive oil. You can experiment with add-ins like seeds, nuts, or dried fruit for texture and flavor. It's a simple reminder that healthy food can be deeply satisfying when made with care—and that your Dutch oven is just as good at baking as it is at braising.

CHAPTER 13

ACCESSORIES AND ADD-ONS

There's something almost magical about cooking with a Le Creuset Dutch oven—it has this ability to make even the simplest meals feel special. But as with any craft, the right tools can make a big difference. Think of your Dutch oven as the centerpiece of your kitchen, the heart of your culinary setup. Around it, you can build an ecosystem of tools and accessories that enhance your cooking, protect your investment, and make everyday tasks smoother, cleaner, and more enjoyable.

Many first-time Dutch oven owners assume that the pot alone does all the heavy lifting—and to be fair, it does a lot. But once you begin cooking with it regularly, you'll notice there are moments when you could use a little extra help: something to stir without scratching the enamel, a trivet to protect your table from heat, or tongs sturdy enough to lift a roast from simmering broth. The beauty of Le Creuset cookware is that it works seamlessly with the right tools—and once you've got a few key accessories, you'll wonder how you ever managed without them.

This chapter explores exactly that: the must-have tools and add-ons that complement your Le Creuset Dutch oven. From utensils designed to protect its glossy enamel to cookware companions that expand its versatility, these pieces will help you get the most out of your investment. Whether you're a beginner or a seasoned cook, knowing what to use (and what to avoid) will make your experience smoother, safer, and far more enjoyable. So, let's dive in and build your perfect Le Creuset setup—one smart tool at a time.

Must-Have Tools and Utensils

When it comes to cooking with enameled cast iron, having the right utensils isn't just a matter of preference—it's a matter of preservation. The enamel coating that gives your Le Creuset its signature look and nonstick performance also needs a little care. Metal utensils, for instance, can scratch or chip the surface, and while that may not ruin your Dutch oven immediately, it can diminish its longevity and beauty over time. That's why choosing utensils made from the right materials is essential.

Start with a good set of silicone or wooden utensils. These are your workhorses. Silicone tools are heat-resistant (often up to 500°F), flexible enough to scrape every bit of sauce from the corners, and easy to clean. Wooden utensils, on the other hand, have a timeless charm and are gentle on enamel surfaces. A simple wooden spoon or spatula can last for years with proper care. Many Le Creuset fans keep both types in their kitchens—silicone for tasks that require flexibility and heat resistance, and wood for gentle stirring and traditional cooking.

A silicone spatula is particularly useful when making soups, sauces, or batters that cling to the sides of your pot. It's perfect for scraping every drop without scratching. For baking enthusiasts, a heatproof whisk with coated wires is another must-have—great for whisking sauces or custards without leaving marks.

Next, you'll want tongs—and not just any tongs. Choose a pair with silicone or nylon-coated tips to avoid scraping the enamel when turning meat or vegetables. They give you precision and control, especially when braising or frying in your Dutch oven.

Another unsung hero of Dutch oven cooking is the ladle. Whether you're serving chili, stew, or a big batch of soup, a ladle with a curved lip makes it easy to pour without dripping down the side. Le Creuset even makes its own line of utensils with silicone heads and stainless steel handles, designed to match both the aesthetic and durability of its cookware.

Then there are the accessories that make handling your pot safer. Because enameled cast iron retains heat so well, you'll need quality oven mitts or pot holders that can handle high temperatures. Thick, heatproof silicone or quilted cotton mitts are ideal. Le Creuset's own "Cool Tools" silicone handle grips are a great add-on; they fit snugly over the handles to give you a safe, non-slip grip even when your Dutch oven is blazing hot.

Finally, don't overlook trivets and spoon rests. A trivet protects your countertops and dining table from the heat of the pot, while a spoon rest keeps your cooking area tidy. Le Creuset's silicone and cast iron trivets are not just functional—they add a pop of color to your kitchen that complements your Dutch oven perfectly.

In essence, having the right utensils isn't about clutter—it's about control. The right tools help you cook confidently, knowing that every stir, scrape, or pour is safe for your Dutch oven and precise for your recipe. Think of them as extensions of your hands—small but mighty helpers that keep your Le Creuset in top shape for years to come.

Silicone vs. Wooden Spoons: Which Is Best?

Ask ten Dutch oven owners which utensil material they prefer, and you'll probably get ten different answers. Both silicone and wooden spoons have devoted fans, and for good reason—they each have unique strengths. The key isn't necessarily choosing one over the other but understanding when and how to use them.

Let's start with silicone. Silicone spoons and spatulas are the modern cook's best friend. They're flexible yet sturdy, able to bend just enough to scrape along the curved interior of your Dutch oven without leaving a trace. High-quality silicone utensils can withstand extreme heat—often up to 500°F—making them ideal for stirring sauces, sautéing, or even baking. Unlike wood, silicone doesn't absorb flavors, oils, or moisture, which means it won't retain odors or stain easily. It's also dishwasher-safe, which is a blessing for anyone who loves to cook but dreads the cleanup.

Silicone spoons shine when cooking sticky or rich dishes—like tomato sauces, curries, or stews—where you might need to scrape the sides frequently. Their smooth, non-porous surface glides effortlessly and prevents food from clinging. They also come in a variety of colors and shapes, often with ergonomically designed handles for comfort.

However, silicone isn't perfect. Some cooks find that it lacks the tactile feedback that wood provides. Because it's so smooth and lightweight, it doesn't give you the same "feel" of the food as you stir. And while silicone utensils are heatproof, their handles—if made from plastic or metal—may not be. Always double-check the manufacturer's specifications before using them for high-heat cooking.

Now let's talk about wooden spoons—the old-world classic that never truly goes out of style. There's something undeniably satisfying about the weight and warmth of a wooden spoon in your hand. Wood provides a natural grip and tactile control that many cooks prefer, especially for stirring thicker mixtures like doughs, risottos, or caramelized onions. It allows you to feel resistance as you stir, helping you sense when a sauce is thick enough or a roux is just right.

Wooden spoons are gentle on enamel, silent against the pot's surface, and—when cared for properly—can last for decades. The key to maintaining them is simple: never soak them for long periods, and avoid dishwashers. Instead, wash them by hand with mild soap and water, then dry them thoroughly. Occasionally rubbing them with mineral oil will keep the wood conditioned and prevent cracking.

Where wood falls short is in maintenance and versatility. It can absorb strong odors (like garlic or curry) and may stain over time. It also shouldn't be left in the pot while cooking, as it can warp or even burn if exposed to heat for too long.

So, which is best? The answer depends on your cooking style. If you love modern convenience, easy cleaning, and precision, go for silicone. If you value tradition, control, and the tactile joy of cooking, wood might be your ideal match. In truth, most seasoned Le Creuset users keep both on hand. Silicone for high-heat stirring and scraping, wood for slow, meditative cooking—each serving its purpose beautifully.

Ultimately, what matters most isn't the material itself but how it complements your rhythm in the kitchen. When used thoughtfully, both silicone and wooden spoons will help you protect your Dutch oven's enamel and elevate your cooking experience.

Recommended Cookware Companions

While your Le Creuset Dutch oven can do almost everything—from searing to baking—it doesn't have to do it all alone. Pairing it with the right cookware companions can make your kitchen more versatile, efficient, and harmonious. Think of these items as the supporting cast that helps your Dutch oven shine in every role.

A great place to start is with Le Creuset's cast iron skillet. If your Dutch oven is the heart of your kitchen, the skillet is its right hand. It excels at quick, high-heat tasks like searing meats, crisping vegetables, or making cornbread. Because it shares the same enameled surface, it's easy to clean and requires no seasoning. Many cooks use their Dutch oven for braising, then move to the skillet for reducing sauces or finishing dishes under high heat.

Next, consider a Le Creuset braiser. While similar to a Dutch oven, the braiser is shallower with sloped sides, making it ideal for dishes that require more surface area—think pan-roasted chicken, paella, or vegetable gratins. It complements the Dutch oven beautifully, giving you flexibility when cooking multiple components of a meal.

Another invaluable companion is the Le Creuset stoneware baking dish. Whether you're baking lasagna, roasting vegetables, or preparing dessert, these dishes distribute heat evenly and retain it well, just like your Dutch oven. They also transition seamlessly from oven to table, adding that signature Le Creuset charm to your presentation.

If you enjoy soups, stews, or stock-making, a Le Creuset stockpot is worth adding to your lineup. It's lighter than cast iron but still sturdy, with an enamel-coated steel body that heats quickly and holds large quantities of liquid. You can prepare big batches of broth or chili while using your Dutch oven for another dish—an efficient setup for meal prep or entertaining.

And let's not forget about accessories for baking. The Dutch oven is famous for making beautiful artisan bread, but pairing it with a banneton (proofing basket), bread lame, and parchment liners can elevate your results. The proofing basket helps shape your dough, the lame gives you those professional bakery-style slashes, and parchment makes for easy transfer in and out of the pot.

Beyond cookware, there are small but mighty additions that make daily use easier. A Le Creuset lid stand helps you safely rest a hot lid without risking scratches or burns. Silicone trivets, as mentioned earlier, are essential for protecting surfaces. And if you love entertaining, Le Creuset's mini cocottes—small individual-sized Dutch ovens—are a delightful way to serve soups, desserts, or side dishes directly from the oven to the table.

Lastly, consider Le Creuset's stainless steel line. The pots and pans in this series complement your Dutch oven beautifully, especially for boiling, sautéing, or preparing sauces. Their mirror-polished finish and even heating make them a practical and aesthetic match for your enameled cast iron pieces.

Choosing the right companions isn't about building a collection for the sake of it—it's about creating harmony in your kitchen. When your tools work together effortlessly, cooking becomes a smoother, more enjoyable process. Every dish transitions seamlessly from one pot to another, every task feels intentional, and your kitchen evolves into a cohesive space where creativity thrives.

CHAPTER 14

CARING FOR YOUR LE CREUSET FOR LIFE

There's something special about a Le Creuset Dutch oven that makes it feel less like cookware and more like a part of your kitchen's story. It's not just another pot—it's a piece that often becomes an heirloom, quietly carrying memories of Sunday stews, winter braises, and slow-simmered sauces. When you invest in a Le Creuset, you're not just buying an enameled cast iron pot; you're committing to a companion that, with the right care, can last a lifetime and beyond.

Unlike cheaper alternatives, Le Creuset Dutch ovens are built to endure decades of cooking. But that kind of longevity doesn't come from durability alone—it comes from how you treat it day after day, year after year. Caring for it properly ensures it stays as dependable and beautiful as the first day you unboxed it. The glossy enamel, the solid heft, the even heat—it all continues to perform flawlessly if you take a few consistent steps.

In this chapter, we'll explore the essential habits that preserve your Dutch oven's quality, discuss what to do if it ever needs repair or restoration, and consider the emotional side of ownership—how this timeless piece can become a symbol of shared meals, traditions, and family. Your Le Creuset isn't just cookware; it's a vessel for your culinary history. With proper care, it can outlive trends, outlast modern gadgets, and one day become something you proudly pass on to someone else.

Long-Term Maintenance Habits

The secret to keeping your Le Creuset in peak condition isn't complicated—it's consistency. The little things you do each time you cook add up to decades of performance. Think of maintenance as a gentle rhythm of use, clean, and store.

First, always allow your Dutch oven to cool before washing it. Rapid temperature changes are the enemy of enamel, especially if you've just finished a long braise or roast. Rinsing a blazing-hot pot with cold water can cause thermal shock, which stresses the enamel and may lead to fine cracks or crazing over time. Instead, let it rest for ten or fifteen minutes. Use that time to enjoy your meal—your Dutch oven will still be there when you're ready.

When it comes to cleaning, stick to mild dish soap and warm water. A soft sponge or nylon brush is ideal for removing residue without scratching the glossy interior. Avoid scouring pads or steel wool entirely; they can leave microscopic abrasions that dull the finish. If you ever encounter stubborn bits of food stuck to the bottom, fill the pot with warm water and a spoonful of baking soda or dish soap. Let it soak for about 15 minutes, then use a non-abrasive brush to gently loosen the residue. This simple ritual keeps your enamel smooth and bright.

Be sure to dry your Dutch oven thoroughly before putting it away. Moisture, especially if trapped under the rim or lid, can create mineral spots or faint discoloration over time. You can let it air dry or towel it by hand—either way, make sure no dampness remains. It's also a good habit to store the lid slightly ajar, allowing airflow inside the pot. This prevents any musty odor from developing if it's stored for a while.

For the exterior, especially those vibrant, signature Le Creuset colors, occasional polishing goes a long way. A dab of mild cleaner or even a mixture of baking soda and water can restore shine to the enamel. Wipe gently in circular motions and rinse with warm water. If you prefer, Le Creuset sells its own enamel care cream that helps maintain the original luster and remove minor stains or dullness.

Even the best cookware benefits from a little routine check-up. Periodically inspect the rims, handles, and lid knob for any chips or cracks. A small nick on the rim won't affect cooking performance, but if enamel chips start appearing on the cooking surface, it's best to address them early. While the enamel is tough, it's not indestructible, and catching issues early helps preserve its structural integrity.

And finally, remember to treat your Dutch oven with the same respect you give any high-quality tool—don't use it for tasks it wasn't meant for. Avoid deep-frying at extreme temperatures or using metal utensils that can scrape the surface. Small habits like these are the quiet guardians of longevity. Over time, you'll come to see these steps not as chores but as gestures of appreciation toward something that makes your kitchen life easier and more beautiful every day.

Warranty, Repairs, and Restorations

Le Creuset's reputation for durability isn't just talk—it's backed by one of the most generous warranties in the cookware industry. When you purchase an authentic Le Creuset Dutch oven, it comes with a lifetime warranty that covers manufacturing defects and workmanship issues. That means if your pot ever chips, cracks, or discolors due to a flaw in production—not misuse—it can often be replaced or repaired at no cost.

To take advantage of the warranty, it's a good idea to register your product on Le Creuset's website after purchase. Doing so makes future claims easier and ensures you're in their system. If a problem arises—say, enamel cracking or chipping under normal use—contact Le Creuset customer support. They'll typically ask for photos of the damage and proof of purchase before assessing whether it qualifies under warranty.

However, it's important to understand what's *not* covered. Damage caused by overheating, metal utensil scratches, or thermal shock doesn't fall under warranty since those are considered user-related wear and tear. But that doesn't mean your Dutch oven is beyond help. Le Creuset offers restoration and recycling programs in some regions, allowing you to trade in or refurbish older pieces. Even if a pot has seen better days, many can be brought back to life through professional cleaning or re-enameling services—though these are typically handled through third-party specialists rather than directly by Le Creuset.

If you ever experience a minor issue, like a loose lid knob or a small chip on the exterior enamel, there are simple at-home fixes. Replacement knobs are available from Le Creuset and can be easily installed with a screwdriver. As for small chips, while they can't be "repaired" per se, they can be smoothed with fine sandpaper to prevent sharp edges and protect the surrounding enamel from further damage. For larger cracks or missing enamel patches on the cooking surface, though, it's best to stop using the pot until it's inspected professionally.

One of the joys of owning Le Creuset is that the company truly stands behind its products. Even decades-old pieces can be evaluated for service or replacement. Many long-time owners share stories of pots passed down through generations being repaired or replaced with newer models. That kind of commitment says something powerful about the brand's philosophy: they don't see their cookware as disposable; they see it as a legacy worth preserving.

If you're ever uncertain whether your Dutch oven's condition warrants professional attention, err on the side of care. Take photos, reach out to Le Creuset support, and describe what happened. They'll let you know the best next step. In a world where most products are designed to be replaced rather than repaired, that kind of customer service feels refreshingly old-fashioned—and it aligns perfectly with the spirit of a pot meant to last a lifetime.

Passing It Down: Making Your Dutch Oven a Family Heirloom

Every scratch, every deepened patina on your Le Creuset tells a story—the kind that no brand-new piece of cookware can replicate. Maybe it's the pot you used to make your first homemade soup, the one that simmered on the stove through countless winters, or the dish that always appeared at family gatherings. Over time, your Dutch oven becomes more than just an object; it becomes a symbol of comfort, love, and nourishment.

Caring for it with that perspective transforms maintenance into meaning. When you clean it gently, when you store it properly, you're not just extending its life—you're preserving its stories. You're making sure that years from now, when your child or grandchild lifts the lid for the first time, they'll still smell the faint hint of stew or bread baked long ago.

Passing down a Dutch oven might sound sentimental, but it's deeply practical too. Unlike digital gadgets or trendy appliances, enameled cast iron doesn't age out of usefulness. It remains timeless, a constant companion no matter how cooking styles evolve. The key is to prepare it for its next chapter just as carefully as you would maintain it for your own use.

Before passing it on, give it a thorough clean and inspection. Make sure the enamel is intact, the lid fits snugly, and the interior remains smooth. If it's been well-used, consider polishing the exterior or replacing the knob so it feels both classic and renewed. You might even write a short note—detailing its history, the meals it's seen, or a favorite family recipe that's always been cooked in it. Including that story gives the piece emotional weight, turning it from a kitchen tool into a family treasure.

In many ways, this is what Le Creuset was always meant to be: enduring, beautiful, and filled with memories. Its craftsmanship bridges generations because it represents something rare in modern life—quality that lasts. Think of all the hands that have lifted its lid before yours and the ones that will after. Each generation adds a new layer of experience, a new recipe, a new memory.

And perhaps that's the quiet power of a Le Creuset Dutch oven. It reminds us that good things—like slow cooking, shared meals, and well-made tools—are worth preserving. With just a little care, your Dutch oven can tell your family's culinary story for decades to come. The aroma of Sunday stews, the sound of a loaf crust cracking open, the laughter shared around a table—all of it lingers in the pot's history, waiting for the next cook to add their chapter.

CONCLUSION

If you've made it this far, you've probably realized something wonderful — your Le Creuset Dutch oven isn't just a piece of cookware. It's a partner in your kitchen adventures, one that's built to last, built to teach, and built to inspire. From your first simple stew to a lovingly baked loaf of bread, this pot quietly becomes part of your rhythm, your routine, and your story.

Le Creuset has always stood for more than craftsmanship — it represents the art of slowing down and savoring. When you lift that heavy lid and breathe in the aroma of something simmering slowly, you're reminded that good food doesn't rush. It develops. It transforms. And just like a well-loved Dutch oven, your skills, confidence, and creativity grow with every meal you make.

Throughout this book, you've learned how to care for your Dutch oven, how to use it to its full potential, and how to create dishes that bring joy to the table. You've discovered that heat retention and enamel coating aren't just marketing terms — they're what make your meals rich, consistent, and comforting. You've learned to appreciate the details: the steady simmer, the golden crust, the gentle scrape of a wooden spoon against enamel. These are the small, sensory moments that make cooking with a Dutch oven so special.

But beyond technique, there's something deeper at play. Cooking with a Le Creuset Dutch oven is an experience that connects you to tradition — a legacy of care and craftsmanship that began nearly a century ago in a small French foundry. Every time you cook, you become part of that story. You're keeping alive the simple but powerful idea that food is meant to nourish not just the body, but also the soul and the people we share it with.

And perhaps that's the greatest lesson this book could offer — that mastery in the kitchen doesn't come from fancy gadgets or complicated recipes. It comes from patience, curiosity, and love. The Dutch oven just happens to be the perfect companion for those qualities. It's forgiving when you're learning, reliable when you're confident, and versatile enough to grow with you over a lifetime.

So don't save it for special occasions. Pull it out on a Tuesday night when you're craving comfort. Use it to whip up a quick one-pot meal, bake a loaf of bread on a lazy Sunday, or experiment with something completely new. The more you cook with it, the more it becomes yours — seasoned not by oil, but by memory.

You'll notice small changes over time. The enamel might lose a bit of its shine. The handles might show faint signs of wear. But that's not a flaw — that's character. It's proof of a tool well-used and well-loved. It's the story of family dinners, quiet evenings, and recipes that worked (and maybe a few that didn't). A Le Creuset Dutch oven doesn't just endure; it evolves right alongside you.

And when you care for it properly, it will outlast you — ready to be passed down, ready to start again in another kitchen, cooking new meals for new memories. That's what makes this cookware timeless. It's not about trends or colors; it's about legacy, the kind that smells like soup on a winter afternoon and feels like home.

So as you close this book, don't think of it as an ending — think of it as a beginning. You now have the knowledge, the confidence, and the inspiration to make your Le Creuset Dutch oven part of your everyday life. Keep experimenting. Keep tasting. Keep creating.

And most of all, keep cooking with joy. Because every time you lift that lid, you're not just making a meal — you're creating something that will be remembered long after the plates are cleared.

APPENDICES

Appendix A — Temperature Conversion Chart

A ready reference for oven and stovetop conversions. Use the chart below when a recipe lists temperatures in Celsius, Fahrenheit, or Gas Mark.

Oven temperature conversion

Celsius (°C)	Fahrenheit (°F)	Gas Mark (UK)	Typical Use
90°C	195°F	—	Very low — gentle warming, slow proofs
110°C	230°F	¼	Very slow roasting, keeping food warm
120°C	250°F	½	Very slow braises, gentle finishing
140°C	285°F	1	Slow roasting, delicate baking
150°C	300°F	2	Slow braises, longer bakes

160°C	325°F	3	Slow roasts, example: pot roast
170°C	340°F	3–4	Low roasting, cooling breads
180°C	350°F	4	Everyday roasting & baking
190°C	375°F	5	Roasting chicken, casseroles
200°C	400°F	6	Roast vegetables, higher temp bakes
220°C	425°F	7	Fast roasts, crust development
230°C	450°F	8	Artisan bread with oven-spring
240°C	465°F	9	Quick sears, pizza-style bakes

260°C	500°F	10	Very high heat — careful use only

Quick stovetop heat guide (relative settings for most electric/induction ranges)

- Low: simmers, melts, poaches (approx. 1–3)

- Medium-low: gentle simmer, slow cooking (3–4)

- Medium: most sautéing and frying (4–6)

- Medium-high: searing and browning (6–8)

- High: quick boil, high-heat searing (8–10) — use sparingly on enameled cast iron

---

Appendix B — Cooking Times & Heat Levels Guide

Practical target temperatures and time ranges you'll want for common ingredients when using a Dutch oven. Remember: the Dutch oven holds heat — check early and expect slower changes.

Meats (braise/roast in a Dutch oven)

- **Beef chuck (braised):** 2½–3½ hrs at 150–160°C (300–325°F) until fork-tender.

- **Short ribs (braised):** 2½–3 hrs at 150–160°C.

- **Pork shoulder (pulled):** 3–4 hrs at 150°C (300°F) or longer for fall-apart texture.

- **Whole chicken (roast):** 60–90 mins at 190–200°C (375–400°F) — sear first stovetop if browning desired. Internal temp 75°C (165°F).

- **Leg of lamb (roast):** 1½–2 hrs at 160–175°C (325–350°F) for medium. Internal temp 60–65°C (140–150°F).

Poultry (braise/poach)

- **Chicken thighs (braised):** 35–50 mins at 160–170°C (325–340°F).

- **Poached chicken breasts:** gently simmer 12–15 mins in aromatics; rest before slicing.

Fish

- **Whole fish or fillets (braise/poach):** 8–20 mins depending on thickness at low simmer (about 80–90°C / 175–195°F). Fish cooks quickly — watch for opacity.

Vegetables

- **Root veg (roasted):** 35–50 mins at 200°C (400°F).

- **Winter squash (roasted halves):** 40–50 mins at 190–200°C.

- **Roasted tomatoes / ratatouille:** 35–50 mins at 180–190°C (covered then uncovered).

- **Steamed/poached greens:** 2–6 mins at gentle simmer — add at end to avoid overcooking.

Beans, lentils & whole grains

- **Dried beans (soaked):** 1–1½ hrs simmering (longer for older beans).

- **Dried beans (unsoaked):** 1½–2½ hrs; check often.

- **Lentils:** 20–40 mins depending on type.

- **Quinoa:** simmer 12–15 mins, then rest 5–10 mins.

- **Brown rice:** simmer 35–45 mins, rest 10 mins.

- **Polenta (stovetop):** 30–45 mins, stirring occasionally.

Bread & baking

- **No-knead bread (preheated Dutch oven):** 30 mins covered at 230–240°C (450–475°F), then 10–20 mins uncovered until deep brown.

- **Casseroles / mac & cheese:** 25–40 mins at 180–200°C (350–400°F) until bubbling and golden.

Frying & oil temperatures (use a thermometer)

- **Light frying (vegetables):** 325–350°F (160–180°C).

- **Pan frying / shallow fry (chicken cutlets):** 325–350°F (160–180°C).

- **Deep frying:** 350–375°F (175–190°C) — do in small batches; use heavy Dutch oven with thermometer and do not overfill.

Notes on timing:

- Cast iron retains heat — once at temperature, reduce heat slightly from what a thin pan would use.

- Always test doneness early; finishing times can be shorter because of residual heat.

- For slow braises, prefer lower temp for longer time for more tender results.

Appendix C — Cleaning Cheat Sheet

Quick, practical steps for the most common cleaning situations. Keep this printed near your sink.

Daily care (best practice)

1. Let pot cool ~10–20 minutes (avoid thermal shock).

2. Rinse with warm water; add mild dish soap and use soft sponge or nylon brush.

3. For stuck food, fill with warm soapy water and soak 10–30 minutes.

4. Rinse and dry thoroughly. Leave lid ajar for airflow if storing.

Stains & discoloration

- **Light stains:** baking soda paste (bicarb + water), sit 10–20 mins, gently scrub.

- **Tough brown/black residue:** boil water + 2–3 tbsp baking soda for 10–15 mins, cool, then scrub.

- **White mineral deposits:** simmer equal parts water + vinegar 10 mins, rinse.

- **Oil build-up:** warm water + a few drops of degreasing dish soap, soak, and scrub. Rinse well.

Burnt-on food (do this before scrubbing aggressively)

1. Cover burnt area with warm water, add 2 tbsp baking soda; bring to a simmer for 10–15 mins.

2. Turn off heat, cool slightly, then gently scrape with a wooden or silicone spatula.

3. Repeat soak if necessary.

Odors

- Rinse, then fill with warm water + 1 tbsp baking soda and sit covered overnight. Rinse next day.

Dishwasher?

- Occasional dishwasher use is *possible*, but **not recommended** regularly — detergents and heat can dull exterior enamel over time.

What *not* to do

- Do not use steel wool, metal scouring pads, or abrasive powders.
- Do not immerse a hot pot in cold water or place on a cold surface.
- Avoid bleach/chlorine-based cleaners.
- Don't store acidic foods long-term in the pot.

Storage quick rules

- Dry fully.
- Store with lid slightly ajar (paper towel wedge) to allow airflow.
- Cushion if stacking: use soft cloth or pan protector between pieces.

Appendix D — Resources & Further Reading

A curated list of resources to deepen knowledge, find recipes, or get support. These are evergreen categories—look for the most updated editions, websites, or local retailers as needed.

Books (recommended reading)

- Books on cast iron and Dutch oven cooking (look for authors who write practical, technique-first cookbooks).

- Regional braising & baking books for deep dives into slow-cooked regional dishes.

- Bread baking books on no-knead and artisan techniques.

Websites & online communities

- **Official manufacturer site** — product care guides, warranty info, replacement parts.

- **Cooking education sites** — technique articles on braising, searing, and baking in Dutch ovens.

- **Active forums and social communities** — for recipes, troubleshooting, and community-tested tips (Reddit communities for home cooks, Facebook groups focused on cast iron/Dutch oven cooking).

- **Recipe blogs** that specialize in one-pot meals, artisan bread, and braises—great for inspiration and step-by-step photos.

Tools & accessories (where to look)

- Manufacturer's accessories (replacement knobs, lids, silicone tools).

- Cookware retailers for braisers, skillets, and compatible trivets.

- Specialty baking suppliers for bannetons, lames, and parchment for Dutch oven bread.

Video learning

- Look for short, focused video tutorials on: preheating a Dutch oven safely, deglazing technique, no-knead bread workflow, and deep-cleaning methods. Videos are especially helpful for pacing (how to test oil shimmer or sear technique).

Troubleshooting & warranty support

- Keep proof of purchase and register cookware when possible.

- Manufacturer's support pages often include claim forms, care videos, and FAQs.

- Local authorized dealers can often help with repairs, replacement parts, or advice.

Quick Reference — Pocket Cheat

- **Preheat empty pot?** Only for bread — heat in oven. Never preheat empty on high stovetop.

- **Searing temp?** Medium to medium-high; oil should shimmer, not smoke.

- **Simmer temp?** Low to medium-low — gentle bubbles.

- **Cool→Wash?** Let rest 10–20 minutes.

- **Stuck food:** soak warm water + baking soda, then gentle scrape.

- **Storage:** Dry, lid ajar, cushion if stacking.

Printed in Dunstable, United Kingdom